Life in the Balance

Life in the Balance

*A Physician's Memoir of Life, Love,
and Loss with Parkinson's Disease
and Dementia*

THOMAS GRABOYS, MD,
with PETER ZHEUTLIN

UNION SQUARE PRESS
An imprint of Sterling Publishing Co., Inc.

New York / London
www.sterlingpublishing.com

STERLING and the distinctive Sterling logo are
registered trademarks of Sterling Publishing Co., Inc.

Library of Congress Cataloging-in-Publication Data Available

10 9 8 7 6 5 4 3 2 1

Published by Sterling Publishing Co., Inc.
387 Park Avenue South, New York, NY 10016
© 2008 by Thomas Graboys and Peter Zheutlin
Distributed in Canada by Sterling Publishing
c/o Canadian Manda Group, 165 Dufferin Street
Toronto, Ontario, Canada M6K 3H6
Distributed in the United Kingdom by GMC Distribution Services
Castle Place, 166 High Street, Lewes, East Sussex, England BN7 1XU
Distributed in Australia by Capricorn Link (Australia) Pty. Ltd.
P.O. Box 704, Windsor, NSW 2756, Australia

Book design and layout: Oxygen Design

Manufactured in the United States of America
All rights reserved

Sterling ISBN-13: 978-1-4027-5341-1
         ISBN-10: 1-4027-5341-1

For information about custom editions, special sales, premium and corporate
purchases, please contact Sterling Special Sales Department at 800-805-5489
or specialsales@sterlingpublishing.com.

Dedication

*This book is dedicated to
my wife, Vicki Tenney Graboys,
to my two indefatigable daughters,
Penelope and Sarah,
and to the memory of
Caroline Rigby Graboys*

*Never deny a diagnosis, but do deny
the negative verdict that may go with it.*
—Norman Cousins

Contents

Foreword

TO THE THOUSANDS OF PATIENTS who came under Tom Graboys's care over the more than three decades of his cardiology practice, Tom was much more than a doctor; he was a trusted adviser, a confidant, and a friend. Rare was the patient who left his office not feeling better than when they came in, for Tom had a way of infusing hope and optimism about the future and easing the emotional burdens of illness. He used words with care. He reassured. He allayed anxiety. He listened attentively. He gave every patient his home phone number, and many used it.

I first met Tom in 1985, when I went to work for an organization cofounded by his mentor, Bernard Lown, called the International Physicians for the Prevention of Nuclear War (IPPNW), winner of the 1985 Nobel Peace Prize. Tom was active in both IPPNW and its U.S. affiliate, Physicians for Social Responsibility. It was hard not to be in awe of this very handsome, brilliant doctor with a strong social conscience.

In the 1990s, my father, a physician himself, had heart problems and was about to undergo a second angioplasty when I urged him to travel from New Jersey to see Tom for a second opinion. My father never had that second angioplasty; indeed, he might not have had the first had he seen Tom from the outset. Tom assured my father that his condition was eminently manageable without surgery, and that lifted an enormous burden of worry from my father's shoulders. From his first visit, and after every annual visit that followed, my father would remark to me that Tom was everything a fine physician should be. My father would know: He was a deeply beloved pediatrician with an extraordinary gift for endearing himself to children and allaying the anxieties of their parents with his quiet, unassuming, deeply human touch. He and Tom were cut from the same cloth.

In 1998, I accepted a position as Executive Director of the Lown Cardiovascular Research Foundation, associated with the Lown Cardiovascular Group, of which Tom was the director. There I saw for myself what an extraordinary physician he was, and how profoundly gifted in the art of interpersonal communication. Both before and after undertaking this book with him, I spoke with dozens of his patients, and I read the hundreds of deeply moving, heart-rending letters patients wrote to him when Parkinson's and the dementia associated with his Parkinson's forced his premature retirement from medicine.

Even in Boston, a city renowned for its legions of exceptionally skilled clinicians, Tom stood out. His clinical judgment was impeccable, his opinions valued by colleagues and patients, his meticulousness unparalleled. But what truly set Tom apart was his uncommon humanity, his intense concern for what ailed the hearts *and* the souls of his patients, and his unstinting generosity with his time. Despite the crushing workload he carried on his shoulders, no patient was ever rushed and no patient concern was ever belittled. A patient's annual follow-up with Tom always ran for an hour or so, unheard of in this era of managed care. After each examination, Tom would sit, knee to knee with the patient, on a small sofa in his office and talk. He never interposed his desk. He treated you as his equal. He was a full partner in your care, and you were glad to have him in your corner. A lot of doctors talk about the importance of the human connection between doctor and patient, but Tom walked the walk.

Tom believed that to be an effective physician, you must first and foremost be a skilled listener. He could learn as much about what ailed you by listening to you talk as he could by listening to your heart with his stethoscope. He understood, and believed in, the healing power of a strong doctor-patient relationship. He was never glib with his advice, whether to lose weight, to stop smoking, or to exercise. He knew that without his constant support and gentle, nonjudgmental follow-through, ninety-nine percent of such advice would soon be forgotten. He accepted gladly his share of the burden to ensure that patients did their best to get or stay well. He spoke easily with patients about subjects that many doctors avoid. He was at ease with discussions of sexuality, for example, and thereby put patients at ease discussing this most intimate of subjects. Many heart patients fear that sex might trigger a heart attack, but Tom believed that sexual intimacy with a loving partner was essential to a sense of well-being and happiness that is beneficial to the heart. He believed deeply in medical science, which he mastered, but he also believed in the power of the human touch, what Bernard Lown has called "the lost art of healing."

When you saw Tom Graboys, you were seeing the best. But Tom never conveyed arrogance. For Tom, each patient was a privilege, a window into the human condition, and he never took your trust for granted.

Though his specialty was cardiology, he treated the whole person. He embraced each individual's complexity. He eschewed pat answers and bromides. He exuded warmth and compassion. As I said, his specialty was cardiology, but really it was people. He was uncommonly generous and compassionate, and was truly beloved by his legion of patients.

When Tom first informed his patients that he had Parkinson's, in August 2004, and when he was forced to retire from practice a year later, he received an avalanche of letters and cards that bear eloquent testimony to Tom's extraordinary impact on the lives of many, many people. I want to let a few, whose sentiments were echoed repeatedly over countless letters, speak for themselves here.

Sal DeSimone was a patient of Tom's for almost thirty years; indeed he was one of Tom's very first patients. He, too, suffers from Parkinson's now. "You impressed me right from the beginning," he wrote. "You have what Socrates called *arête*—the excellence of the soul." The letter was signed "your friend and patient."

"We have known each other for almost thirty years," wrote Virginia Richardson, another longtime patient. "You gave me the hope to do what I've had to do, enjoy life when I could and overcome adversities. I am fully aware and appreciative of the time, thought, and care you have applied to me, as a person and patient."

"So many people love you for so many reasons," wrote patient Kenneth Wile, who is also a physician. "You have the rare ability to envelop patients, the families and their loved ones and provide them with a sense of comfort, confidence and hope. You exemplify the qualities that medical schools try to imbue in their students and that physicians work a lifetime to achieve. Thank you for your tender care over the past twenty-three years. You have helped redirect my paths in life and have added hope and joy to my journey."

"I want you to know that the caring questions you always asked about my life's difficulties, while not eliminating them, comforted me by the simple act of a doctor's caring enough to ask," wrote Pamela Perry.

And, finally, this: "Your [retirement] letter has brought me what my Swedish ancestors called 'soul sickness,'" wrote Raymond Kask. "It's deeper than being 'heart sick.' You were and are more to me than my cardiologist. You were my younger brother, my friend, and you had all the time in the world. It was your way of showing you care. Now I want you to know that I care for you."

It seems especially cruel, both to Tom and to all those who came to depend upon him, that at the age of sixty-two, a particularly insidious form of Parkinson's disease, one accompanied by a syndrome called Lewy body dementia, forced him to retire from medicine. That someone as devoted as Tom to the health and well-being of others for all of his adult life must now endure the cruel and unremitting trials of dementia is beyond reckoning.

When Tom asked if I would help him write this book, I knew it would be an experience like no other in my life. Unable to write, battling cognitive difficulties and progressive dementia, Tom needed someone who might, he hoped, be able to listen and then to communicate his most intimate thoughts and feelings. Aside from raising my children, never have I been entrusted with such an awesome responsibility. Like everyone who had known Tom over the years, it was painful for me to see what Parkinson's had done to him. And the task was particularly challenging because Tom's ability to organize and articulate his thoughts has been compromised. But knowing Tom as I have over the years proved invaluable in our collaboration. I knew something about the essence of Tom Graboys before we ever met to discuss this book; and that, I think, is what made it possible for us to communicate and collaborate effectively.

Working with Tom has given me the rare privilege that so many patients allowed Tom, a window into the human condition. I doubt I will ever see such grace in a human being again.

This book is one tough read, because what ails Tom is unrelenting and merciless. Every day is filled with extraordinary challenges and with terror about what the future holds. Yet, in spite of it all, there were plenty of flashes of Tom's dry, ironic humor. One day in December 2006, when we weren't quite halfway through our work on this book, I invited Tom to a Boston College basketball game, a short walk from his house. Tom had been telling me for months about how Parkinson's and dementia affected nearly every detail of daily living and his ability to navigate the world, but this was the first time I had a chance to see him outside the familiar environs of his home. During the game, he tried, without success, to make sense of the numbers on the scoreboard. I introduced him to the people we were sitting with, but he had difficulty remembering who they were from one moment to the next. At halftime, we got up to head to the snack bar, and Tom faltered as a sudden drop in blood pressure had him groping for a wall for support. When that passed, I watched as he fumbled awkwardly with his money, not quite sure which bill to use while trying to pay for some M&Ms, and struggled to peel back the lid on his hot chocolate. Then, aware that I was watching him, he looked at me with the small smile that I had come to associate with his moments of self-deprecating humor and said, "This is like a field trip for you, isn't it?"

Tom has suffered two enormous tragedies in the past decade: the loss of his first wife, Caroline, to cancer in 1998, and the loss of much of himself to Parkinson's and Lewy body dementia. A lesser man would have curled up and rolled away long ago. Yet Tom, despite the anger, frustration, and sadness that have been visited upon him, remains a deeply sensitive person determined to derive from his life as much happiness and pleasure as he can, a resilience that is positively breathtaking. And he remains acutely sensitive to those around him—family, friends, and former patients he encounters in regular visits to the Lown Center, where he still maintains an office. No less remarkable was his determination to tell his story so that others might find some comfort—or inspiration or validation—in their own struggles, whether with Parkinson's, dementia, or another affliction of the mind or body.

It took enormous courage and fortitude, given the toll Parkinson's has taken physically, mentally, and emotionally, for Tom to write this book. But it is the logical continuation of a life devoted to caring for the world, one human being at a time.

When Tom and I discussed how this book—a book with more than its fair share of anguish and tragedy—should end, I suggested to Tom that he imagine what Dr. Tom Graboys the physician might say to Tom Graboys the Parkinson's patient if they were sitting knee to knee on the sofa in his small office, because Dr. Tom Graboys would find a way to convey hope, optimism, and an appreciation of all that it means to be truly alive in whatever time and space is given to us.

—Peter Zheutlin

Preface

TO KNOW WHO I AM TODAY, losing control of my body and my mind to an insidious form of Parkinson's disease, you have to know who I was fifteen years ago.

In 1993, Boston Celtics star Reggie Lewis grabbed a rebound and was headed upcourt during an NBA playoff game against Charlotte when he slumped to the floor and blacked out for a few seconds, before getting to his feet and making his way to the bench. When Lewis returned to Boston, the Celtics assembled a team of twelve Boston-area cardiologists with various specialized expertise to determine if Lewis's fainting episode indicated a cardiac problem. This team of top physicians was soon dubbed, rather extravagantly, "The Cardiology Dream Team" by the Boston media. I was one of them.

Though the evidence was ambiguous, the team concluded that Lewis might have suffered a particularly dangerous type of arrhythmia, an irregular beating of the heart, caused by cardiomyopathy, a disease of the heart muscle. If correct, that diagnosis meant Lewis's basketball career was over.

Based on a second, more favorable opinion rendered by another eminent cardiologist who is a dear friend of mine, Lewis resumed playing basketball. Then, in July of that year, Lewis, just twenty-seven years old and in his prime, collapsed while shooting baskets at a local gym and died.

I was forty-nine in 1993 when I was a member of the Cardiology Dream Team. I had a beautiful wife, Caroline, and two wonderful daughters. I was on the faculty of Harvard Medical

School and the staff of Boston's Brigham and Women's Hospital. I had a thriving private practice with the Lown Cardiovascular Group, led by the inestimable Bernard Lown, widely regarded as one of the most accomplished cardiologists of the twentieth century, and with whom I had trained after medical school. I was, to use a well-worn cliché, on top of the world in every way. I was blessed.

Today, I can no longer see patients or give rounds. My face is often expressionless, though I still look younger than my sixty-three years. I am stooped; I shuffle when I walk; and my body trembles. My train of thought regularly runs off the rails. Though I am remarried to a lovely, caring woman, Vicki Tenney Graboys (the former Vicki Baker), an accomplished interior designer, Caroline, the mother of my children, my soul mate for more than thirty years, is gone. She lost her life to colon cancer in 1998.

I have lost an awful lot in the past ten years: a spouse, a career, and, to a considerable degree, control over my body and my brain. Used to being a caregiver, a healer to a legion of patients, I have lost countless relationships with people I once cared for. For a long time, while I was in denial about the severity of my condition and the extent of my impairment, I expended extraordinary physical and mental energy trying to maintain the façade that I was the in-control doctor. My patients didn't want to leave me, but in the end I had to leave them—for their own good.

People always want to read stories of triumph over tragedy. But there is no sugarcoating Parkinson's and, as the baby boomers age and live longer, more and more of us are succumbing to the disease. There is no silver lining here. There is anger, pain, and frustration at being victimized by a disease that can, to some extent, be managed but cannot be cured.

While Parkinson's, which is caused by a chemical imbalance in the brain, is usually understood to be a disease characterized by loss of control over body movements, most people afflicted with the disease also experience difficulties with attention, concentration, problem-solving, concept formation, sequencing, vision, depression, and memory. But a significant portion of Parkinson's patients—and I am one of these—have an associated degenerative disease, known as Lewy body disease or Lewy body dementia, which seriously impairs cognition and has other powerful side effects, such as hallucinations and violent REM sleep, that can result in injury to oneself or one's sleeping partner. By night, I can suddenly lurch out control; by day, I feel as though I have an on-off switch that controls my brain and I am not in control of it.

Named for the doctor who discovered them, Lewy bodies are abnormal protein deposits. When they form in a particular area of the brain stem, they deplete the neurotransmitter dopamine, which then results in Parkinsonian symptoms. In Lewy body dementia, however, these abnormal proteins are spread throughout other areas of the brain, including the cerebral cortex. Though Lewy bodies themselves are a factor in all Parkinson's cases, Lewy body disease changes the Parkinson's equation dramatically. Patients with ordinary Parkinson's can expect to live to their full life expectancy. Lewy body disease, the progression of which is variable and unpredictable, can cut life short and dramatically affect quality of life. Mine is not an easy life, and it is certainly not the life I, or my family, imagined for ourselves, nor did we ever think we would experience it.

Despite all that I have lost, I continue to derive pleasure from my life. Regular exercise and yoga have been indispensable in helping me achieve some sense of well-being and have helped me maintain some control amid the chaos inflicted by my brain. I still play the drums occasionally in a band comprising local doctors. Most importantly, I have grandchildren now and have been lucky enough to find love a second time with Vicki.

Writing this book, telling this story of a degenerative neurological disease from the inside out, is an act of defiance. I have good days and bad. On the best days, when I come out of the clouds, I have brief periods when I am sharp. But on others, I falter and am keenly aware of what is happening. Parkinson's has taken some of my eyesight, and I cannot sit at a computer and type anything longer than an E-mail—and even that requires considerable effort and concentration. My memory often fails, and trying to organize my thoughts is often impossible. To tell my story, I had to find someone who could bring some order to my thoughts and put them into words.

I have a great sense of urgency about this book. My disease is a degenerative one. I may not be able tomorrow, or next week, or next year, to tell my story. I live with the knowledge that the theft of my mind may not be over and that this story would then be lost forever. Just as I am not the person I was fifteen years ago when I was a member of the Cardiology Dream Team, I may not be the person next year, or even next month, that I am today.

Why share this painful and tragic story publicly? Why go

through the effort? Why summon up once again the various losses I have endured along the way? Why subject my family to the public sharing of the most intimate details of our lives?

Well, I am a doctor. I have spent my entire adult life caring for people. And unlike much of what the medical profession has become in this age of industrialized medicine, our practice at the Lown Group was a throwback to a time when doctors listened at length to patients and sought to treat the body *and* assuage the soul. My engagement with patients was deeply personal. Medical school trained me to care for the heart, an organ profoundly affected by the stresses, strains, and anxieties of daily living. But to be truly effective, I listened as people told me their life stories, their fears, and their hopes. Such deep engagement with patients is therapeutic for the patient and an invaluable aid to the doctor. From thousands of patients over nearly four decades, I learned much, for each patient is a window into the human condition. That is why a doctor should feel privileged by all patients who entrust themselves to his or her care.

Even though I am no longer able to engage with patients or to teach young medical students, this book is a logical extension of my medical career. Parkinson's now afflicts more than one and a half million Americans, with sixty thousand more cases diagnosed each year; and an estimated 640,000 Americans *under the age of sixty-five* (not to mention the millions over sixty-five) are suffering from dementia caused by Alzheimer's and other causes, such as Lewy body disease. By sharing this story, it is my hope that others who suffer from serious disease, especially those struggling with diseases that steal control of mind or body, along with their loved ones, will find some comfort—that I may be able to articulate and, therefore, validate what they feel and experience but may not be able to express. This book is the only way I know to continue, in a sense, to be a doctor. This isn't an easy story to tell. But it is an important one.

—Thomas B. Graboys, MD

ONE

My Days

NOTHING IS SECOND NATURE to me any more. No task is too simple, no activity so routine that I can do it without forethought. Is the glass right side up, or will I pour orange juice all over the counter again? When I leave the kitchen to walk to the bedroom, how will I get there? At the party tonight, where will the stairs be, and how will I navigate them? Will I be able to join the conversation? Or will I be standing in a corner, nearly catatonic?

For social gatherings, I have what I call my cassettes: a repertoire of conversational riffs on various subjects that will allow me to enter the conversation and, with luck, appear to be a reasonable facsimile of the old Tom Graboys. Can I pull it off? Can I act the part and mask the reality of dementia? One of my goals in social situations is to have people go away saying, "You know, Tom seemed pretty good." It allays the anxieties of friends and colleagues when you look and sound good, even if they cannot fathom the effort it took to muster such a performance.

Without my cassettes, entering a group conversation is like trying to get on the freeway traveling at twenty miles an hour while the traffic is rushing by at seventy. Slowness, an all-encompassing mental and physical slowness, has descended upon me. It is not going to lift.

* * *

Holding on. Much of my life, today and every day, is about holding on to what I've got—or, more precisely, holding on to what is left. There is still happiness in my life: my wife, my children and grandchildren, music, and, now that I can no longer practice medicine, the time to explore new interests such as indoor cycling and writing. There are even days when the "old Tom" emerges, usually briefly, and I feel like my old self, only to awake the next day and come face-to-face once again with the reality of life with a progressive neurological disease.

For now, I still see the light; but on the other side of this knife-edge ridge I walk, there is darkness, so I hold on. I have discussed this with my wife and adult daughters. There is a point beyond which I do not wish to go. That is the day I can no longer control my bowels and my bladder, a common problem for patients with advanced Parkinson's disease. To me, this is the ultimate regression. I have been in too many hospital wards and nursing homes where patients with severe dementia are lying on the floor or sitting in their own urine and feces, oblivious to the world around them. I have seen the end of this road, and I won't go there.

I am determined not to let Parkinson's, which has stolen so much, steal my dignity. That is what I am really holding on to. Dignity. It's why I exercise, practice yoga, and play the drums. It's why I shave every day. It's why I dress well and make sure I look my best. As a cardiologist with a predominantly geriatric patient population, I often noted in my files when a patient started look-ing unkempt, a look that signaled that he had surrendered, been beaten down, or no longer cared enough to pull himself together. I no longer save my best clothes for special occasions. Now, *every* day is a special occasion.

* * *

The daily struggle with Parkinson's disease, especially in this form, is relentless. There is no reprieve, and the future is uncertain. Even on the good days, Parkinson's lurks like an unwanted shadow. On the bad days, my frustration boils over into anger and despair.

In my case, Parkinson's is a twenty-four-hour-a-day affair, because the associated Lewy body disease brings forth vivid nightmares and violent sleep on a weekly basis, nightmares so realistic that I am likely to act them out. I have dreamed of being attacked and, in an effort to fight back, have inadvertently struck my wife, Vicki. This is extremely abhorrent and sorrowful to me, but it is part of the picture of our daily lives.

* * *

In the mornings when I wake, or when I stir from the midday nap that has become as essential to functioning as my medication, I lie entombed in my own body for ten or fifteen minutes. This paralysis of mind and body lasts until enough synapses can spring into action to allow me to move.

As a young intern and resident, and later as an attending cardiologist, I was accustomed to being summoned suddenly in the middle of the night. I could launch myself out of bed, get dressed, and perform at my intellectual peak within moments. I could make life-and-death decisions within seconds of a nighttime phone call. Today, I wait for thousands of tiny cellular engines to start themselves so I can rise from the bed and begin another day, trapped in a body that no longer fully responds to my will and subject to a mind that spins at 33 RPM in a 78 RPM world. Neurologic disarray affects every aspect of my life.

* * *

One small accommodation to my Parkinson's is our master bedroom, located on the ground floor of our home. This is where I begin my day, staring at the ceiling. We're on the ground floor because navigating stairs can be difficult for me. Stairs often appear fused together, navigable only by feel and with one hand firmly on the railing.

The tricks my eyes play on me are not a matter of focus. Objects sometimes appear strangely flat, without dimension. Double vision is a problem. Minor hallucinations from time to time make it hard to trust my own eyes. Many patients with Lewy body disease experience frightening hallucinations, often involving insects or animals. I have been spared such hallucinations so far, though I do sometimes "see" stationary objects move or mistake a pan of brownies for a loaf of bread. Sometimes, while I look at a person or thing, the object of my vision is replaced, just for a split second, with the image of another. The hallucinations are subtle and transient, but disconcerting nonetheless. Wasn't that chair on the other side of the room a minute ago? The occasional auditory hallucination breaks into my day as well. I will hear an alarm, convinced it is sounding, but only I will hear it.

Once liberated from the bed, I head to the kitchen, though I sometimes get disoriented and find myself lost momentarily in my own house, or forget where I was going and why. I pause and wait for the confusion to pass. Such demoralizing mental lapses constantly punctuate my day and tear at my self-esteem.

In the kitchen, I have learned from experience to use my fingers to determine if the glass for my orange juice is right side up before I pour. I can see the glass, but I often cannot process what I see and translate it into an understandable reality. So I make one of what will be countless adjustments during my day to compensate. I move the tip of my finger to the top of the glass. If it strikes a solid surface, I know to turn the glass over. If my finger meets no resistance where the top would be, I know the glass is right side up. If my medication hasn't "kicked in," I concentrate as hard as I possibly can to pour the juice into the glass with trembling hands.

The common perception of Parkinson's as little more than body tremors is way off the mark. In his poignant and courageous memoir, the actor Michael J. Fox put a very public face to Parkinson's. Fox's predominant symptom, which is controlled with medication, is hyperkinesia—extravagant, involuntary body movements and tremors. But in many cases, like mine, the symptoms are global. No major function of mind or body has been spared. From visual perception, cognition, and speech to blood pressure, body temperature control, and sexuality, Parkinson's permeates every aspect of my being.

I have the classic appearance of a Parkinson's patient. I often appear hunkered down, head bowed, shoulders slumped, my once-fluid body rigid, my once-graceful gait an old man's shuffle. This has been hard to accept, for I have a strong narcissistic streak. My looks have always been important to me. I always believed that my interpersonal skills and my attractiveness (attested to by my wives) were largely responsible for my success in life. So I am trying to hold on to my looks too.

The dyskinesia, or lack of body control, is especially pronounced as I dress. Indeed, it would be more accurate to say "I do daily battle with my clothes" than to say "I get dressed in the morning." The once-simple task of putting my arm through a sleeve can be exasperating, and Vicki will often turn to see me on the losing end of a wrestling match with my clothing. Buttons are a particular challenge—fine motor skills have become an oxymoron in my life—and I don't have the balance to put my pants on standing up. The simple act of dressing in the morning is a physical and mental challenge and a constant reminder of the regression wrought by Parkinson's.

This lack of motor control, along with my now-slurred speech, is the source of many embarrassing moments. People may sometimes quite logically assume that I am drunk. At the end of a recent airplane trip, I attempted to put on my overcoat while standing in the aisle and ended up looking as though I were frozen in a straitjacket. Temporary paralysis is yet another symptom of my Parkinson's. It was surely a strange sight to those watching me on that plane, but to me it was just another in a series of moments of public humiliation to which I have become more accustomed over time.

The simple act of carrying a cup of coffee to a cash register and trying to find the money to pay for it can be a daunting challenge, one made even more difficult because if people are waiting behind me, I feel great pressure to perform. My trembling hands cause the coffee to slosh about, and I fumble for the change in my pocket, change that often ends up on the floor. Sometimes I cannot tell a nickel from a dime from a quarter, so I hand over my change like a child at a candy counter and wait for the clerk to sort it out. At the supermarket, I can never figure out which way to slide the debit card. More than once I have had a cashier snatch it from my hand abruptly, point to the people behind me, and say, "People are waiting, sir!" Who wants to turn around and announce, "I have Parkinson's disease"? So you swallow the small indignities and humiliations and try ahead of time to think about each tiny step in the process of a task as simple as buying a carton of milk.

In my cardiology practice, I often discussed with patients what physicians call "ADLs," the activities of daily living. In assessing the toll of any disease, an important measure is how it impacts the patient's ADLs. By that standard, the toll of my Parkinson's has been great. The most routine tasks require a level of attentiveness and concentration that I once reserved for the treatment of seriously ill heart patients.

The physical manifestations of Parkinson's go well beyond tremors and involuntary jerks of hands and arms. Balance is problematic. Last year, I fell in the shower, hitting my head and drawing blood. As a result, I am more defensive and deliberate in my movements. I am always anticipating what obstacles—stairs, furniture, inclines, curbs—I will have to navigate in the places I go. I am constantly in a high state of vigilance that is draining, both emotionally and physically.

The impact of Parkinson's is so pervasive that even my thermo-regulatory system is out of control. I often feel too hot and too cold simultaneously. Hot flashes accompanied by sweats send me to the shower two or three times a day. A hot bath is often the only way to get comfortable again.

My hands and face often tell the story. While my face may be perspiring uncontrollably, my hands can be clammy and cold. As a practicing physician, I always paid careful attention to my patients' hands, often beginning my physical exam there, for the hands often provide important diagnostic clues. Thickened tendons in the palm can indicate diabetes. Swelling of soft tissue near the fingertips combined with nailbed changes may be a sign of lung cancer or cardiovascular disease. Painful lumps in the fingertips can suggest an infection of the heart valves.

But there was another, equally important, reason for beginning a physical exam with the hands: taking the patient's hands in your own invites intimacy and trust, a nonthreatening beginning to an exam that will involve physical contact between physician and patient. An examination of the hands can also yield clues to a patient's state of mind or tell you something about their life that can provide an easy entrée to conversation. Are the patient's hands moist with sweat? If so, the patient may be anxious. Do they tremble? If so, Parkinson's may be suspected. Are they yellow with nicotine? Then the patient smokes. Do they reflect hours spent in the garden? If so, the patient may be put at ease with a question about his or her garden. My hands, too, reveal much. They are often red, often cold, and they often have a life of their own. My hands tell you a lot about my Parkinson's.

Another "small" problem related to the hands is what doctors call "micrographia," which is typical of Parkinson's patients.

No matter how hard I try, the amplitude of my handwriting gets smaller and smaller as I write because my hand muscles fatigue. This is, in fact, no "small" problem because with memory failing, I often leave notes to myself, ironically notes that I cannot later read. It's not unusual for me to write the same note six or seven times before I produce one legible enough to be read hours later. It takes me ten times as long to write a note as it once did. This is one of the daily frustrations that can quickly raise a high titer of anger. I have crumpled countless pieces of paper in frustration and thrown them at the wall. This is how Parkinson's chips away, bit by bit, at your humanity and the sense of normality that all seriously ill patients crave.

Sudden hypotension, usually lasting only a few seconds, is another symptom of my Parkinson's. Typically triggered by exercise or exertion of some kind, these sudden drops in blood pressure bring me to the brink of fainting. My peripheral vision disappears and narrows to tunnel vision as I begin to lose consciousness. Frequent hydration is a prophylactic, so I try to remember to drink six to eight glasses of fluids a day.

Eating is yet another ADL that has suffered the impact of Parkinson's. In addition to the mess I often make at my place, I have to avoid some foods that I once enjoyed because I can no longer manipulate my silverware well enough to cut a steak, for example, and I detest the notion that someone will have to cut up my food for me as if I were an infant or a senile old man. This can be especially embarrassing at a restaurant or dinner party. If it were not for the fact that Vicki has become a swift and very discreet monitor of the area around my dinner plate, it would often appear that a three-year-old child had been seated at my place. The more dramatic tremors associated with Parkinson's can be controlled with medications; yet the compromise of fine motor skills can turn a formal dinner into a management nightmare as I try to move soup from bowl to mouth without spilling it all over my shirt, or try to confine rice to the boundaries of my plate.

The rigidity of body and loss of physical control and fine motor skills have also interfered with some of my favorite activities. Though I still play the drums, a passion for many years, I can no longer coordinate my feet sufficiently to generate the rapid motion of cymbals needed for jazz, and imparting rhythm—and drums are all about rhythm—is increasingly difficult. Drumming is becoming harder for another reason as well: Math is an essential part of music—whole notes, quarter notes, tempo—and I can no longer process mathematical relationships. Sheet music simply doesn't make sense to me as it once did.

Loss of physical control also means occasional drooling, sometimes when I am awake, but more often during sleep. When I wake up, I find that I have soaked the pillow with drool and the sheets with sweat. If I've had a good day the day before, waking up like this the next morning is an unwelcome reminder that Parkinson's is my constant companion.

Each of these manifestations of Parkinson's, no matter how trivial, erodes my sense of stability and my desperate need to feel that there is stasis—that I have battled Parkinson's to a standoff, at least temporarily. The appearance of any new symptom invariably leads to the inescapable conclusion that the disease is progressing.

* * *

Physical deficits are only one part of my daily battle with Parkinson's. My interactions with people are marked by a slowness of thought (called bradykinesia) that is as embarrassing as it is frustrating. It's more than losing my train of thought, though that happens a hundred times a day or more; it's having the words in my head, but being unable to move them from the part of the brain where thoughts are formed to the part that controls speech. The neural pathways are disorganized, like some fantastically complex highway system with overpasses and intersections, on-ramps and exit ramps, all leading nowhere. A thought forms, it gets sent down the pike, only to get lost in some cul-de-sac where it spins like a whirling dervish. The train of thought in such cases isn't lost; I'm well aware of the thought; but I cannot maneuver it to the place in my brain that will allow communication. Sometimes the thoughts will finally spin out of the cul-de-sac and find expression; often, however, they simply spin themselves out like a spent whirlwind, never escaping. The halcyon days when I spoke eloquently and with great confidence are gone. As I said, nothing, not even speech, is second nature any more.

It is this dementia, this progressive loss of cognitive and intellectual functioning, that is the hardest symptom of my disease to live with and the hardest to accept. I can no longer balance a checkbook or calculate a restaurant tip. The concentration required for two hours of often-halting conversation leaves me weary. A veil descends, like a night canopy over a birdcage, and I need to nap to recharge my diminished synapses. Many Parkinson's patients will tell you that having Parkinson's is like having a switch in your head, a switch that is not in your control; a switch that can be flipped up and down once an hour or ten times in a minute. Sometimes I simply shut down and wait out the power outage.

I have lost large chunks of knowledge that have dropped away like a glacier cleaving huge chunks of ice into the sea. It's still hard for me to admit to having dementia, because there are times, wonderful moments of lucid, clear thought, when I feel intellectually intact. I try desperately to hold on to those moments, or hours, but inevitably they pass. Am I an intellectually intact person with bouts of dementia? Or am I a demented person with moments of lucidity?

Predictably, this cognitive decline has led to a loss of intellectual and social confidence. Initially, my social confidence was completely destroyed by Parkinson's. Because stress and a high volume of sensory input exacerbate the slowness of mind that frustrates me so, I resisted social occasions for a long time. But Vicki has rescued me from life as a recluse. She has always had an active social life with a wide circle of friends, and there are countless charitable functions on her calendar. Though social events are challenging on many levels, they force me to engage with the world, as difficult as that engagement can sometimes be.

When a friend of Vicki's recently graduated, as an older student, from Wellesley College, we were invited to a buffet dinner on Wellesley's magnificent campus. It was so crowded that you could hardly move, so noisy you could barely hear. My anxiety always spikes at such times. Sensory overload makes it harder to mask the symptoms of Parkinson's. The pressure to "perform" feels onerous and quickly becomes counterproductive. I couldn't muster the motor coordination to move food from the buffet table to my plate; conversation, for several reasons, was impossible. The verbal sparring, the quick give-and-take that is so much a part of daily life, no longer takes place on a level playing field for me. For one thing, Parkinson's interferes with voice modulation, so I often speak, involuntarily, in a near-whisper. The volume of my voice is one indicator of how I am feeling: On my good days, it can be close to normal; when I'm struggling, it can be inaudible. Competing with the background noise at a party when my voice is faint is arduous, and I am often forced to lean in and speak inches from people's ears. Gradually, I have grown more comfortable explaining to people, even those I don't know, why I may be hard to hear and telling them to feel free to tell me if they can't hear me. The playing field is also tilted because I am keenly aware that I am often well off the pace of the palaver. I often drop fancy words like "palaver" into my conversation to prove I still have "it," that I am not an intellectual shipwreck. Words I once thought pretentious I now use deliberately in conversation, to compensate for the loss of intellectual firepower.

When we return home from these occasions, I am always eager for a debriefing from Vicki. "How was I?", I want to know. This is a part of holding on: I am relieved when the report is a good one—that I may have started slowly, but picked it up by evening's end. When I'm off, it's terribly discouraging.

Because I am always on the alert for any sign of deterioration in my condition, when Vicki tells me that I seem confused,

I am instantly thrown into a state of acute stress, wondering if this is the moment when I fall off, irrevocably, to the dark side of the ridgeline I walk. From years of experience listening carefully to patients and even listening between the lines for what my colleague Bernard Lown calls "the unarticulated ache," I have become quite astute at sensing anxiety in others. Often Vicki doesn't need to say anything: I know, just from looking at her, how the evening has gone.

* * *

Fifteen years ago, I taught a course at Harvard Medical School on heart disease and sexuality. Sexuality is a topic widely ignored by physicians for a variety of reasons, including the physician's discomfort with the subject. At the time, most cardiologists weren't even raising the issue of sexuality with their patients—yet almost every heart patient I saw would bring the subject up eventually, if I didn't. Most wanted to know if sexual activity was safe for them. And more often than not, my reply was that not only was it safe; it was necessary. The course of heart disease can be dramatically affected by stress and the strength of personal relationships. Patients in relationships filled with anger, resentment, and guilt are at greater risk than those in relationships that bring comfort, joy, and peace. For married patients, or those in a long-term relationship, a healthy sex life marked by intimacy and caring can impart a sense of well-being, reduce stress, and bring happiness.

The effect of Parkinson's on my own sexuality has been profound. But, similarly to heart disease cases, sexuality is the forgotten part of the Parkinson's discussion unless initiated by the patient. The issue of sex and Parkinson's is a complex one, in part because the medications used to treat the symptoms of Parkinson's, including the characteristic depression, can affect sexual function. Some antidepressants and other medications can cause impotence, for instance. It's an example of how, in diseases like Parkinson's, or Alzheimer's, or multiple sclerosis—diseases of the central nervous system—everything can affect everything else. It's like an ecosystem—a change in one niche can trigger changes throughout the system.

When Vicki and I first met, we were in our mid-fifties and enjoyed an active sex life that brought great intimacy and closeness to our marriage. After my Parkinson's diagnosis, various medications were prescribed in a search for a combination that would bring my symptoms under control. As a physician, I was well aware of the complexity of "polypharmacy." I frequently saw patients on multiple medications for the treatment of multiple ailments, often with inadequate consideration given to how the individual medications would interact. At its worst, polypharmacy with inadequate consideration of drug interactions can be life-threatening. It took some experimentation until I responded favorably, but Zoloft, prescribed for depression, seriously depressed our sex life.

At one point, I became so frustrated that, without telling Vicki, I abruptly stopped taking the Zoloft. A good doctor is not necessarily a good or compliant patient. (Indeed, as we will see, though I was a good doctor to my patients, during the onset of Parkinson's I was a terrible doctor to myself.) When, weeks later, I confided to Vicki that I had taken myself off the Zoloft, she was justifiably angry. She already felt that I had betrayed her trust, in the months before our marriage, when I had assured her that my fainting spells and other early warning signs of Parkinson's were under control and not serious. Winning back her trust was still a work in progress, and I had just dealt that work a setback. And quitting the Zoloft intensified my Parkinson's symptoms. It was a Catch-22, for Parkinson's symptoms themselves interfere with sexuality, and so do the medications used to treat it.

I resumed the Zoloft, and slowly, after much open and honest discussion, we regained some of our intimacy, though it has been inconsistent. But Parkinson's and the medications used to treat it continue to have profound effects and permeate every aspect of our lives.

I suspect that most neurologists who see Parkinson's patients see sexuality as incidental in the face of such a devastating disease, a bit like worrying about a cold in a patient with terminal lung cancer. But for the patient living with Parkinson's, the patient who has already lost so much, sexual intimacy can be especially meaningful and a vitally important quality-of-life issue. Ironically, in the 1990s, I served on the FDA panel that oversaw the approval of Viagra. Such drugs can play a critical role in giving back to Parkinson's patients—and to others who suffer from sexual dysfunction resulting from neurological disease—a part of their humanity.

* * *

Every day, something happens—some event large or small—that triggers my anger at what has happened to me. The anger, too, is pervasive. I am angry over my losses, angry about the terrible pain and anxiety my illness has introduced into the lives of my wife and daughters, angry at the loss of much of my sexuality, angry that my young grandchildren will never know "Pops" without dementia, angry that it takes me twenty minutes to change a lightbulb, angry that the disease has ripped apart the fabric of my life, and angry at being dependent. Parkinson's has foisted on me a dependence on Vicki that I resent, but one that has become absolutely necessary. Every day, she anticipates my needs even as she struggles with her own fears about what might lie just ahead.

Yet, though I chafe at my dependence, I know that I am far healthier for having Vicki in my life. Her own vigilance eases the road I travel. When I flew to California alone to visit my daughter a few months ago, I was filled with anxiety about the logistics I would have to manage. The ticket counter, the hustle and bustle of the airport, the security line, the boarding process—it all seemed overwhelming. When I travel with Vicki, I know it will all be taken care of, from the packing of my suitcase, to the car, to the seat assignment. It's a double-edged sword, of course. I *am* dependent. I *am* face-to-face with how I am compromised with Parkinson's at times like that. Yet having someone tend to all these details removes a major source of stress.

And Vicki isn't the only one. People are forever helping me in small ways—making things easier for me is how people respond to my illness, helping me as I fumble to put on a seat belt, for instance, or as I try to slip my feet into the foot straps on an indoor spin bike.

* * *

Every day, I take my own measure: Is it getting worse? What will the future bring? Can I hold on? Can I live my life with the current level of dementia? How much loss can I accept? When these questions threaten to take hold of me, I use yoga discipline and literally try to move them aside; for the questions are unanswerable, the answers unknowable.

After the existential questions, the one that persists most cloyingly is whether this disease has taken from me the last remnants of being a physician. Throughout my adult life, my identity has been inextricably linked with being a doctor, a caregiver, a healer. Today, my stethoscope, the accoutrement that more than any other identified me as a physician, is gathering dust, and I know I will never wear it again. Unable to attend to patients, I had to ask whether holding on—by keeping current with the major journals, attending grand rounds, or appearing at hospital meetings—made sense. Even sitting still, a task made difficult by muscle cramps brought on by Parkinson's, was making it impossible to sit through grand rounds and meetings. Besides, would I merely be clinging to my unrecoverable past, a sad shadow of my former self? Did I have anything left to contribute? Am I a real doctor any more? At times, I feel guilty that I can no longer care for the thousands of patients who were depending on me. Accepting that I can no longer practice puts me face-to-face with the reality of who I am now.

* * *

Nearly every day, I see—or talk by phone with—friends, family, and colleagues who ask, "How are you doing, Tom?" They mean well, of course. These are people with hopes for me, and they want me to know that they care. But each time the question is asked, I am reminded of how much has been lost. What can I say to this question? "Fine," is my usual reply, but I am not fine. I would rather find out how *they* are, how *their* kids are, what's happening in *their* lives. I want them to see that Parkinson's has not made me self-absorbed. I want the conversation to show them that I took a huge neurological hit and that I'm still standing. But the normality that almost all people with a serious illness crave is forever beyond my reach.

* * *

To hold on, to try to maintain the status quo, I constantly monitor myself for signs of decline. But I am hardly passive, and I do not accept the inevitability of further decline, even though I know, intellectually, that it is likely. I believe that I can at least slow the pace as long as I don't surrender, and writing this book was one way of not surrendering. Though I could not write it without help, the intellectual engagement required by the process was a way of exercising mental muscles. To keep my body fit, I exercise regularly. Spinning classes have boosted my energy and my sense of well-being, as has yoga. And though I deeply regret no longer being able to practice medicine, I now have more time to focus on my own well-being.

Despite the myriad symptoms and problems that I have to struggle with every day, I am optimistic that I can keep my situation stable. I believe this because I have to believe it. I have to believe that tomorrow can be as good as today. That is the most that I hope for.

TWO

Do They Know?

ON SEPTEMBER 21, 2005, I wrote a letter to my patients. The letter was part surrender and part release, and it signaled the end of a ferocious struggle to maintain a façade of normality as Parkinson's disease cut deeper and deeper into my body and my mind. In the letter, I told my patients, many hundreds of them, some in my care for more than thirty years, that I could no longer be their doctor.

Being a physician was everything to me. I had spent all of my young adult life preparing to be a physician, and all of my adult life being one. It was the reason I got up in the morning. It was an integral part of my identity and my sense of self-worth. It was the symbol of everything I once had been—decisive, quick-thinking, analytical, and in control—but could no longer be.

I was trained, and by personal inclination and temperament was drawn, to a style of medicine that has largely gone by the wayside. My patients will tell you that their care was not simply a matter of tests, diagnoses, and prescribed remedies; it involved a sharing of fears and hopes, anxieties and triumphs. I firmly believe that an intimate, caring doctor–patient relationship is more than common decency; it has important therapeutic value. Sharing a patient's burdens, listening (the most important diagnostic tool in medicine), and assuring are as valuable as—if not even more valuable than—the impressive array of technology at our disposal. There were many complex reasons why I fought so hard to stave off "retirement," a word I have come to detest, but one of them—no, perhaps a thousand of them—was knowing what it might mean for each patient who had invested so much in me and who had entrusted their lives to my care. Each of them will find another excellent cardiologist; but trust and friendship—words patients used over and over again in their letters to me after learning that I was being forced to retire—are not so easily replaced.

I can't say, exactly, how long I fought to keep up the illusion of normality as Parkinson's took control of my mind and body. With a progressive disease, the changes can be so gradual that they are hardly noticeable, until one day the cumulative effect is obvious to almost everyone. In my case, especially in the early stages of what would later be diagnosed as Parkinson's, it was also easy to attribute the early symptoms of fatigue and forgetfulness to another trauma in my life, the death of my wife Caroline in 1998.

Caroline's twenty-two-month battle with cancer was an especially grueling and cruel one—for her, for me, and for our daughters: Penelope, then in law school, and Sarah, then in college. It was devastating on every level: physical, emotional, and spiritual. I would lose myself in my work by day, refusing to let up on a demanding schedule of rounds and appointments, and then would take care of Caroline by night in a seemingly endless succession of twenty-hour days. I was drained, spent, exhausted, depressed, and afraid. Guilt weighed heavily. At work I felt guilty that I wasn't doing more for Caroline; at home I felt guilty that I was shortchanging my patients because I was exhausted and preoccupied. And I knew that I was losing my closest friend and confidante, my soul mate since college.

Caroline and I had been together for thirty-five years, since we met at Cornell in 1963. I was the intense Jewish workaholic from the gritty working-class city of Fall River, Massachusetts, constantly stressed by my need to succeed, and very insecure. Caroline was the free-spirited blonde surfer from California, an Episcopalian with a Southern California ease and self-confidence. A perfect match.

Ours was a strong and loving marriage, and her death left me bereft to the core. It would be easy for me—and my colleagues, friends, and patients—to attribute mental lapses, fatigue, or mild confusion to the ordeal and stress of Caroline's death and the grief that followed. By any measure, my workload was enormous, but it became my shelter and my retreat and gave me a reason to keep going. Work was my salvation.

In retrospect, however, some of the subtle changes that I started to experience in the months and years immediately following Caroline's death, such as a resting hand tremor and occasional forgetfulness, were not the ordinary manifestations of extreme grief, but the early expression of Parkinson's disease. Where the symptoms of grief and despair left off and Parkinson's began is impossible to know, but I suspect that they were closely related. Nevertheless, I had a rational and logical explanation for everything that was already beginning to happen to me, one that would allow me to believe that with time the old Tom—sharp, energetic, always on top of his game—would re-emerge. But it was not to be.

* * *

As the symptoms of Parkinson's increased in number and severity over the years, especially the Lewy body dementia, and as a pervasive sense of dread, that something terribly wrong was happening to me, began to take hold, I started to go through every day determined to concentrate, to conceal mental lapses with offhand remarks, to carry myself upright and walk normally even as my posture, which began to droop, and my gait, which gradually became a shuffle, started to succumb to Parkinson's. I didn't yet know that I had Parkinson's, but I was already fighting to mask the reality that was unfolding within, and by day's end I was utterly exhausted from the effort it took to try to play the part of the old Tom.

By the day of my second wedding, to Vicki, in September 2002, the external signs of Parkinson's were still relatively minor and I was able, with some effort, to mask the occasional mental lapses. I knew something more insidious was under way, but I didn't know what.

That I was in serious trouble became clear on the morning of my wedding, when I fainted. Vicki was already alarmed; eleven months before, I had fainted while we were in Bermuda on vacation. We had immediately flown back to Boston, and I had learned that I needed to have a pacemaker implanted. So, when I fainted on our wedding day, I kept it secret from her. It was insane and inexcusable and today I am deeply embarrassed by it, but I did it.

Though not usually the cause, Parkinson's can trigger cardiac syncope, an event that results in a sudden drop in blood pressure and heart rate and a loss of consciousness. Just days after our wedding, on our honeymoon in Mexico, I tripped and fell hard to the ground, bruising my chest. I was beginning to suspect that these episodes were connected to other, subtle changes that I was becoming aware of. Though something very significant was afoot,

I was still in denial and didn't share the depth of my concern with Vicki, though she was beginning to have her own concerns that something was seriously amiss. Concealing the depths of my own concern laid the groundwork for the complex and difficult struggle that has engaged the two of us ever since. Indeed, because Vicki and I only met and started dating near the end of 1999, she actually never knew the old Tom and how much I had already changed.

Shortly after our honeymoon, Vicki and I had dinner with Gilbert Mudge, a prominent Boston cardiologist, and his wife, Bobbi. Unbeknownst to me, Bobbi called Vicki shortly afterward. The Mudges, close friends for many years, were very concerned that something was wrong—it was clear from my demeanor, my conversation, and my countenance, and they were trying to find out from Vicki what was happening; and she, in turn, was trying desperately to figure it out herself.

As 2002 folded into 2003, my symptoms grew more and more pronounced and my efforts to conceal them more desperate. But it would be another year, December 2003, before I would scrawl a note in my diary: "This disease may have begun 2 years or more . . . it is progressive . . . typical of Parkinson [sic]." And it would be almost two full years after that before the combined efforts of my colleagues, my family, my psychotherapist, and my neurologists would breach the wall of denial that I had built and would lead me to the excruciating decision that I could practice medicine no more.

Those three years, 2003 through 2005, were the years of battle—to hold on to my work, to hold on to myself, to simply hold on. The battle, however, nearly did me in, for it demanded so much of me that there were days when I literally had to crawl up the stairs from the garage to the living room at the end of the day, before collapsing on the sofa in a state of complete exhaustion.

At first, I thought I could maintain control by cutting back modestly on my patient load, which had been growing steadily for several years, and which was the most demanding in our group of six cardiologists. Toward the end of 2002 and into early 2003, I did cut back, but just a bit.

It is typical for physicians who have trained in Boston, or who work at the Brigham and Women's Hospital, one of the nation's best, to eschew weakness. The ability to work hard for extended periods under great stress is a valued trait in the Boston medical culture where I had come of age as a physician. Cutting back, even modestly, was a sign of weakness, and it gave me pause. It was also a small concession to the growing sense of unease within. I was desperate to maintain the status quo and to deny that something was wrong, and even this small step nagged at me. But I thought that if I worked, say, ten percent less, I would be that much more effective. Incredibly, I had always assumed that most of my patients denied some of their symptoms, or at least the severity of them; yet, when it was me, I was completely unable to see that I, too, might be engaged in this magical thinking, in which I could make everything right again by just conceding a little.

* * *

Oddly, my denial coexisted with my making private notes about my increasingly troublesome symptoms. For example, on January 2,

2003, I wrote: "Some problem with dictated notes . . . some lapses in word recall . . . tremor has worsened slightly." A few weeks later, on January 23, I scrawled: "Loss of train of [thought]; can picture my response but then lose it . . . at times feeling angry and paranoid. Is this . . . early dementia or Parkinson's . . . I am speaking very softly now."

Yet I publicly continued to refuse to acknowledge that anything was wrong.

* * *

The first person at work to express concern to me about my health was Helene Glaser, a registered nurse with our group. I had worked with Helene ever since I had been a resident at Boston City Hospital more than three decades before. She knows me as well as anyone, and is a keenly observant and fine clinician in her own right.

She knew as early as 2002 that something wasn't right, and she kept a close eye on me, and on my charts and my patients as well: She was watching my back. I rebuffed all of her nettlesome queries about my health: "I'm just tired." That was all that I would concede. And when she persisted, and I realized that she was double-checking my work, I was hurt and angry. I thought she was being overly critical and unfair, and I found her double-checking of my work and her questions about my health infantilizing. I couldn't fathom where her concern—and what I saw as her meddling—was coming from, and I was impenetrable on the subject. My relationship with Helene, rock-solid for so long, began to falter.

Then came a moment, early in 2003, that I will never forget. I was in the parking garage underneath the Brigham one day when a voice called to me from a short distance away. It was Martin Samuels, chairman of the Neurology Department at Harvard Medical School and Brigham and Women's Hospital. He knew nothing of the drama unfolding in my life, but he said to me, "Tom, who is taking care of your Parkinson's?" I was stunned. I hadn't even been diagnosed with the disease, though I feared I might have it, and I had thought I was effectively concealing my undiagnosed symptoms. Yet Martin knew just from looking at me. I mumbled something dismissive, got in my car, and headed for home. I was numb.

By this time, the occasional resting hand tremor that had been noticeable for several months had become more pronounced, my posture had become more stooped, I moved with more deliberation, and the titer of my own concern was escalating, as was that of my colleagues—Drs. Bernard Lown, Shmuel Ravid, Charles Blatt, and Brian Bilchik. When my colleagues told me that they strongly felt I should consult a neurologist, I was ready to do so. But I was far from ready to quit the practice of medicine or admit that I was growing increasingly ill.

* * *

Dr. John Growdon is a nationally renowned neurologist, an expert in Parkinson's, at Massachusetts General Hospital, and Professor of Neurology at Harvard Medical School. I liked Growdon right away. He has a generous laugh and, in his bow tie and tweed jacket, he is the very image of Boston medicine.

Growdon noted some mild physical rigidity and slowness of movement, and he recommended cognitive testing and a CT scan before recommending any specific treatment or making a definitive diagnosis. Physicians generally seek the most benign diagnosis for symptoms—or defer a diagnosis—until the evidence is clear. A headache, for example, can be caused by tension or a brain tumor, but one doesn't rush to tell a patient he might have a brain tumor when there is another explanation, both more likely and benign, and there is no evidence of a tumor. When the patient is also a physician, the treating physician may be even more conservative. And it is not at all unusual for a diagnosis of Parkinson's to be delayed until well after the onset of symptoms, even years, for many Parkinson's symptoms are non-specific, meaning there can be many causes.

There was, in fact, another reasonable explanation for my symptoms, a neuro-psychiatric disorder, perhaps related to depression, that could be treated with medications. Had I not been a physician, I suspect Growdon might have rendered a diagnosis of Parkinson's, which he considered, at that time. Indeed, I told him that day that I thought we might be dealing with Parkinson's. But, for now, the symptoms were mild enough and advancing gradually enough that no name was affixed to my condition. Growdon did prescribe several medications to help ameliorate some of my symptoms, primarily depression and anxiety, both common in Parkinson's but obviously symptoms with many possible causes. But that evening I wrote in my diary: "This is a terrible situation."

* * *

Polypharmacy is a clinical challenge for all physicians. Patients with multiple ailments are often under the care of more than one specialist and often take multiple medications. Many conditions require drug cocktails—several drugs used in combination—for effective treatment. In every case where a patient is taking more than one medication, whether prescription or over-the-counter, there is the risk of an adverse interaction. Even herbal remedies, widely regarded by the public as "safe," are themselves drugs and must be considered when weighing the risks of adverse drug interactions. Even when one physician prescribes multiple medications, or even a single medication, it can take some time to determine the dosages and combinations that are right for a particular patient, for drug tolerance varies greatly from person to person.

In my case, the first combination of medications Growdon prescribed was a nightmare, though they generally are very effective and well tolerated by most patients. They plunged me into an unrelenting fog so thick that I could barely function. At times, I was virtually catatonic.

Early one morning, at my psychotherapy appointment with Dr. Susan Block, my therapist for many years, she was so alarmed by the effects of the medications that she insisted that I go straight home and not to the office. Desperate and unable or unwilling still to comprehend the toll both my undiagnosed Parkinson's and this early treatment regimen were taking, I ignored her directive and went instead to the office: Disheveled, incoherent, and with my mind reeling from the effects of the drugs, I saw three patients that day.

Under Growdon's guidance, we tried several drug combinations over many months, each seemingly more debilitating than the next, until at last we found a combination that seemed to alleviate some of my symptoms without the profound side effects. For a short time, things seemed to improve.

But, in early April 2003, I made another note in my diary: "Increasingly difficult to express concepts . . . I am not 'sharp.' Today with [a patient] I paused and could not express [sic]. Felt 'hot' in my neck—that occurs whenever I am in a 'lapse.'" (The heat I felt was caused by relaxation of the blood vessels that accompanies a sudden drop in blood pressure.) The struggle to get through the day, even with a modest reduction in patient load, was getting tougher. I was napping between patients just to summon the energy to get through the next appointment. My concentration began to falter, and it took every ounce of energy I had to try to stay focused. Even so, patients were beginning to ask me if I was okay and to share their concerns with Helene. She, and my assistant for twenty-five years, Claudia Kenney, double-checked my charts, cleaned up my notes, and reviewed every prescription I wrote. Helene was also double-checking every patient's vital signs. She was so concerned that she raised her concerns with some of my colleagues, but they attributed my symptoms to fatigue. They had insisted I see a neurologist, which I had, and he had rendered no specific diagnosis. They appreciated Helene's concerns, but did not, at least outwardly, share them.

Feelings of paranoia, and of concern about my career, began to intensify. I made a note: "Being judged by Helene Glaser and

Shmuel Ravid. Under the gun to perform 'perfectly.' Hanging on fear that they will take my privileges—that would be devastating. My ego could not stand that."

My colleagues were concerned about my performance, but were reluctant, I think, to face up to my deteriorating condition, for understandable reasons. First, on a personal level, they were trying to be as supportive and understanding as possible, and they bent over backward to keep me working. They knew how much practicing medicine meant to me, how essential it was to my psyche and my self-esteem. And I was both the director of the practice and the heir apparent to Bernard Lown, then in his early eighties. I was a valued colleague, and everyone involved had a lot riding on my continuing to lead the group and on my participation in the clinical practice.

But none of my colleagues saw my notes, or were there—as Helene often was—when I examined my patients. I wasn't the only person in the office in denial.

* * *

Just getting through the day was taking a bigger and bigger toll, emotionally and physically, and gradually my efforts to conceal my worsening symptoms were failing.

My speech was slow and halting. Where once I had been able to make multiple decisions rapidly, I became confused and indecisive. I sometimes became disoriented in the office and needed to be reminded where the examining room was. My clinical notes, written and dictated, became increasingly indecipherable. Stress and fatigue, the default explanations for the changes that were now becoming apparent to colleagues and patients alike, were becoming less and less convincing. But I held fast, because I could not bring myself to accept what was becoming obvious: my condition, still undiagnosed, was worsening.

At the end of 2003, I made that note in my diary, "Typical of Parkinson [sic]," and added another on February 11, 2004: "Possible dementia . . . I have begun to realize there is an inevitable aspect. Memory. I am losing it. The essential question is how long I can hold on and compensate for cognitive dysfunctioning [sic]." So, early in 2004 I saw Dr. Growdon again. This time, the diagnosis Growdon and I had hoped to avoid became inevitable.

I shared the diagnosis of Parkinson's with my colleagues, but not, at first, with my patients. We needed time to understand the implications of the diagnosis, which, in and of itself, did not render me unfit to practice. Indeed, now that we knew what we were dealing with, there was every reason to expect that the right drug regimen would allow me to manage my symptoms and continue, albeit on a reduced schedule, to see patients. The initial signs of dementia, we thought, might be attributable to some of the medications I had been taking and would therefore dissipate once a better combination was found.

Indeed, by March 2004 the medications were beginning to help. On March 28, 2004, I noted in my diary: "Spirits better. [Vicki] and I observe stable situation. I feel well, like my old self. Major [improvement] compared to one year ago." But it was not to last; the progression of the disease would soon start to outpace the ability of the medications to control my symptoms.

On May 24, 2004, I wrote in my diary: "Do I detect people talking[?]" I was haunted by a simple question: "Do they know?" "They" were my patients. "Know" referred to the changes that were transforming me. In essence, these questions reflected the extraordinary effort I was making to hold on to the old Tom. I wondered constantly if I was able to convincingly act the part.

But what we didn't know yet was that something even more insidious than the Parkinson's was at work; my downward slide soon accelerated again.

* * *

By mid-2004, my growing inability to articulate my thoughts, and my episodes of confusion, were apparent to everyone; no amount of effort could conceal them. I was indecisive and unable to focus. At the hospital, I sometimes had to spend an hour writing notes in a chart because my handwriting was so poor that it took multiple efforts to render a legible version. Even my car was evidence that something was seriously amiss—on some days, I could no longer maneuver into my usual parking space parallel to the building, and my colleagues would find my car parked at odd angles, blocking passage through the lot. Concerned about me, for my patients, and, understandably, about possible legal liability, they insisted that I revisit Growdon for a re-evaluation and further cognitive test-ing. He would, they said, need to vouch, in writing, for my ability to continue to practice.

In retrospect, I believe my colleagues were surprised by Growdon's conclusion. I know that Helene, Vicki, and my psychotherapist, Susan Block, were surprised. Growdon wrote that I suffered from Parkinson's disease marked by "bradyphrenia," slowness in response time in thinking. But that was not what took everyone by surprise; it was his optimism that drug therapy could provide effective treatment and that with such treatment "Dr. Graboys will be able to continue as an effective physician."

I seized on those words; I was fighting for my job as though I were fighting for my life: In my mind, there was no difference. Life without my work would be no life at all. My white coat and stethoscope defined me. It was simply inconceivable to me that I would ever have to stop being a doctor. This was more than a metaphor about the importance of work in my life; if I were too ill to work, I would have to face a terribly inconvenient truth: that my debility was so severe that I might be facing a life that I wouldn't—or couldn't—live at all. Because without my practice, who was I? The old Tom would be gone forever if I couldn't practice, and I wasn't sure that I could—or would even want to— live my life as the new Tom, mind and body at the mercy of a merciless disease. I simply could not allow myself to consider the possibility that I was no longer fit to practice medicine and all that that implied, so I hunkered down and carried on. I was still not ready to admit that I was seriously impaired, and Growdon's words affirmed that I could still be effective in my work.

After Growdon's letter, addressed to my colleague Shmuel Ravid, who had now assumed my position as director of the clinical practice, I agreed to further reduce my schedule. I could remain effective, I reasoned, if my already-reduced workload were less demanding still.

Two weeks later, in early August 2004, I wrote a letter to my patients informing them, for the first time, that I suffered from Parkinson's, that fatigue was the primary symptom, and that, while I would continue to see patients, my reduced hours might mean that they would have to wait longer for appointments, or might find that my time with them on a given day might have to be more brief than usual.

Many patients who came to see me after receiving that letter told me that they had suspected Parkinson's all along. They had known something was wrong, but very few had been able to voice their concern to me, though some did to Helene. "He seemed distracted," "he seemed preoccupied," and "he didn't seem like himself" were phrases Helene sometimes heard during the days leading up to the letter. It pains me now to think that any patient went away with doubts about my ability to attend to them as I always had in the past, but it is indicative of the extraordinary level of denial I was in that I was surprised that anyone noticed.

The letter was reassuring to most of my patients. They now had an answer to their questions about me and a concrete explanation for their often-unspoken concerns. And since Parkinson's is typically a motor disease and I am not a surgeon, I am aware of only one patient, among many hundreds, who was uncomfortable continuing under my care.

The solace I found in Growdon's letter was short-lived, however, for things rapidly went from bad to worse yet again.

* * *

Even with my substantially reduced workload, I was coming home in the afternoon numb with exhaustion and would pass out cold on the living room sofa. Still clinging to the delusion that I was managing pretty well at the office, one day I asked Helene, "How do you think things are going?" She'd been looking for an opening, unsure how to tell me what she believed was an essential truth—that I had to retire; that I was no longer competent to practice medicine. I was completely taken aback, angered and hurt. But the wall of denial—the "charade," as Helene called it—started to crumble.

* * *

In the early summer of 2005, in the conference room at our Brookline offices, the doctors in our group gathered for one of the most somber and painful occasions in my life. This was a meeting that no one wanted, that everyone dreaded; but it was, in retrospect, the meeting that everyone urgently needed. I was told, gently but firmly, that it was the unanimous opinion of my colleagues that I was no longer fit to practice medicine. I had developed a national reputation in medicine over the years, and no one wanted to see it end badly, first and foremost for the sake of my patients, but for me as well. Many fine physicians have seen a lifetime of outstanding work forever tarnished by one tragic mistake, and my colleagues were anxious for me to retire with my reputation intact.

As painful as this meeting was for me, it was no less painful and traumatic for my colleagues. For Bernard Lown, who had made me his protégé more than three decades earlier and who expected me to succeed him and carry out his extraordinary legacy, it was a tragic day. For others in the group whom I had mentored and with whom I shared so much of life, it was also a heartbreaking day. For me, it marked the end of the only life I had known as an adult. I had no idea what awaited me on the other side of the exit door, and I was filled with dread.

This difficult meeting with all its attendant sadness, and Helene's frank assessment of my condition, were two of the three straws that gradually broke through my fierce denial. The third was an evaluation by Dr. Lewis Sudarsky—a neurologist specializing in movement disorders and a Brigham colleague—which occurred over a series of appointments that began in May 2005 and concluded on July 22 of that year. My daughters, Sarah and Penelope, had been urging a second opinion, and I agreed. Independent cognitive testing recommended by Sudarsky and Growdon, and evaluated later by them, showed profound cognitive impairment, a dramatic change from testing performed just a little over a year before. And Sudarsky had another bombshell for us—the diagnosis of Lewy body disease, the cause of my Alzheimer's-like dementia. (There is no clinical test for Lewy body disease; it is a diagnosis made by observation of symptoms.) This was my worst fear come true, for I have harbored, throughout my adult life, an obsessive fear of Alzheimer's.

In Sudarsky's opinion, one that Growdon concurred in, I had to stop medical practice. The evidence was overwhelming. My colleagues—including Helene, who knew me best—told me it was time to quit. My daughters were urging the same. My therapist, Susan Block, had been gently steering me toward that conclusion as well, trying to navigate around my staunch denial and

protect my fragile sense of self. And now Sudarsky was unequiv-
ocal. Vicki struggled to comprehend how things had gone so
wrong since our wedding day not three years before.

* * *

In early September 2005, the entire Lown Center staff—doctors,
nurses, researchers, secretaries, and lab technicians—gathered in
the conference room on the second floor of our Brookline
offices, the same room where my colleagues had, just several
weeks before, rendered their judgment about my ability to practice. I had presided over countless meetings in this room over the
years. The bookcases are lined with medical texts; photographs
of the dozens of cardiology fellows trained under Bernard
Lown's—and, later, my own—supervision hang on the wall. In
this room I had mentored post-doctoral fellows and medical students, analyzed complex cardiac cases with my colleagues, and
guided the work of the research foundation associated with our
practice. In this room I had indulged my passion for cardiology
and spent countless rewarding hours.

For three years, my growing debility had been the elephant
in the room that everyone saw but few acknowledged.
Apprehension, grief, sadness, fear—in varying degrees, my illness and my struggle to conceal it had affected everyone.
Wearing my white lab coat and stethoscope for the last time, I
told the staff what many already knew: that I was calling it
quits. There were many tears shed that day. The old Tom was
being mourned, and we all wondered what the future would
hold for the new Tom.

* * *

To my great surprise, the day I had been dreading for so long—the day I had fought so hard to prevent—didn't bring with it the sense of defeat and dread that I had feared. Rather, a sense of elation and relief came over me. For three years, I had poured all of the physical, mental, and emotional energy I could muster into denial and pretense, and it had exacted an enormous toll. The charade had demanded so much of me, and had come at such a huge psychic cost, that waking up unburdened brought huge waves of relief. I was out of the closet, and it was liberating.

Of course, the reality is that I am living with a progressive neurological disease that continues to take its toll—emotional, mental, and physical. It is not a quality of life that anyone would envy. But the heavy burden of denial, and the huge expenditure of energy required to try to maintain a façade of normality, had been lifted

* * *

For many years, I served on the Harvard Medical School admissions committee and interviewed hundreds of prospective young doctors. Ironically, one of the questions I had asked of every applicant was this: "You become aware that a colleague, a fellow physician, is suffering from an impairment that gives you concern about his or her ability to practice medicine. You are concerned enough that you worry about the well-being of his patients; that he or she might unintentionally do harm to a patient. What would you do?"

This is the desired answer to that question that I had asked so many times: "I would speak directly to the physician involved and relay my concerns. If necessary, I would speak directly to his chief and his family. The well-being of the patient has to be paramount."

I still believe this is the only correct answer. But in real life, I have learned, it's not so easy; and it may not be obvious, even to another trained physician, when an impairment compromises patient care. Every day, doctors with personal and emotional problems, fatigue, alcoholism, drug dependence, or other illnesses treat thousands of patients. Their disability or problem may not necessarily affect their judgment and their skill. And, as a 2006 issue of the Massachusetts Medical Society's newsletter, *Vital Signs,* stated, "There are no specific, empirically derived guidelines for determining if an impaired physician is fit to return to work."

The Hippocratic oath, taken by every physician since the time of the Ancients, begins: "First, do no harm." But untangling and reconciling the complex emotions, obligations, and moral imperatives when one is dealing with a beloved colleague can make it difficult to navigate to the right decision.

Susan Block put it this way in speaking about me in the summer of 2006, after I retired—but I think she could have been speaking for all of my colleagues and my family as well: "I was extremely concerned about Tom's ability to continue to practice and so aware of his denial and how brittle it seemed. I worried about how to move him to a gracious retirement without breaking him, given the degree to which his identity was connected to his work as a doctor."

I am confident that despite my increasing debility, I did no harm, thanks in no small measure to the highly skilled people it was my privilege to work with. But I also look back and recognize that despite my best intentions, I did not—because I *could* not, in the last two or three years of my working life—attend to many patients with the attentiveness and focus that I had given them throughout most of my career. This is not an easy pill for me to swallow, but I take comfort in the hundreds of letters filled with love, compassion, and support that I consider, more than any award or title, the measure of my life in medicine.

THREE
Love and Marriage

WHEN I FAINTED ON THE MORNING of my wedding in
September 2002, it was, for Vicki, the latest in a series of seemingly inexplicable episodes that had punctuated our courtship.
There was the fainting episode in Bermuda in late 2001, followed
by surgery to implant a pacemaker. There was the fall in the
shower that left my head bleeding. There were nights of violent
nightmares. And then there was the wedding-day fiasco, which
she only learned about shortly *after* the wedding. Through it all,
Vicki relied on me, and my medical expertise, for assurance that
I was okay. And that is precisely what I did: I assured her that
these were unrelated episodes, that they were minor or—at least
in the case of the pacemaker—treatable. I was fine.

But the truth was different, and I had for some time been
harboring a sense of foreboding about my health. Two years earlier, I had confided to a friend that I thought something was
seriously wrong with me, although I didn't know what. But I
had always been neurotic about my own health and fearful
about loss. It would have been natural for me to have had
heightened health concerns after Caroline's death, but my anxiety was qualitatively different this time around.

During our courtship, I had engaged Vicki in a game of
"what if," a game I had been playing much of my life in one
form or another. Throughout my first marriage, for example, I
often asked Caroline what she would do if I became seriously ill.
I needed assurance that she would stick with me through thick

and thin. At an early age, my father had suffered a series of strokes, and my mother lovingly cared for him for many, many years. My father's ill health raised my concern for my own. This could happen to me. Would Caroline be there for me as my mother had been for my dad? Knowing *intellectually* that she would was not enough, because the fear was neurotic.

So it wasn't out of the ordinary for me to ask similar questions of Vicki. *What if* you fell in love and the person told you he was terminally ill? Would you marry him? *What if* you remarried and then learned that your husband had a life-threatening disease? Would you stay with him? It wasn't a conscious effort to find out what might happen to *us* if I were indeed ill, but rather, I told myself, a way to probe Vicki's heart and soul. Who was this person I was falling in love with? What *kind of person* was she? In retrospect, however, I can see that my questions were motivated by my fears about my own health, some that I had carried all my life, some prompted by the sense that something insidious *was* indeed happening to me. Had I been single and met Vicki ten years earlier, I probably would have asked her similar questions, because that was my M.O. But they took on an added sense of urgency when I asked them in 2001.

I still wonder: Had she known that all these seemingly inexplicable events were the early manifestations of Parkinson's disease, if she could have peered around the corner and glimpsed the full extent of what lay ahead, would she have married me? I don't think it's possible for either of us to really know the answer to that question. Today, we both have to believe, and want to believe, that the answer would have been "yes." But that may be because too much has transpired, and too much sweat and too many tears have been shed, to be able to cope with the implications if the answer was "no." What I do know is that because of my failure to share my concerns with her, Vicki was never given a choice; and that has, understandably, been the source of a lot of anger and bitterness, which we have worked through painstakingly.

Not sharing my concerns before our wedding was, in a sense, the original sin in our marriage. It was a sin of omission, not a deliberate attempt to deceive. I was afraid and in denial, aware and unaware at the same time. But it was a sin that would have serious consequences as we coped with my deteriorating health in the months and years ahead. Incredibly, it wasn't until early 2006, almost four years after our marriage, that I first admitted to Vicki that I had harbored serious doubts about my health long before our wedding. It has been hard enough for her to come to terms with the fact that the peculiar events of our courtship were, in fact, harbingers of a disease that has turned our lives upside down. To this day, she wonders: Should she have known? Should she have asked more questions? Did she miss something? For her to learn nearly four years later that I had suspected a serious problem well before our wedding almost cost me our marriage.

What I did was—it's painfully obvious with the benefit of hindsight—unjustifiable and patently unfair. I am, in a very real sense, guilty of a kind of fraud. A good marriage has to be grounded in trust, and this was no way to begin a marriage. Indeed, after I fainted on our wedding day, my daughters, without Vicki's knowledge, rushed me to see Shmuel Ravid to make certain that nothing was wrong with my heart or my pacemaker.

I wince now when I think that I would do such a thing without telling the woman I was to marry later that day. *What was I thinking?* Regaining Vicki's trust has taken great effort, and I have made a solemn pledge: no more surprises. Never again, for example, will I take myself off medications without consulting Vicki and my physicians. And never again will I try to hide anything about my clinical condition and the changes that are under way today.

* * *

When we started dating in late 1999 and early 2000, Vicki wasn't looking to remarry. After a difficult first marriage that had ended in divorce about a decade earlier, she had grown happy in her new life. She was successful professionally, active socially, and completely independent. With aging parents to care for and three young-adult children to shepherd into adulthood, the last thing she wanted was to become caretaker to an ailing husband. Indeed, one of the things she found attractive about me was that I, too, was independent, personally and financially, and self-sufficient. I could *and would* take care of myself.

Vicki, too, is a victim of my Parkinson's. That she has stayed with me, continued to love me, and attended generously to my every imaginable need speaks volumes. But for us both, there is deep, gnawing, and persistent anger, and it has only been through hard work, with therapists and with each other, that we have managed not only to survive the original sin of our marriage, but to have made an imperfect peace, with each other and with the hand fate has dealt us.

* * *

I first met Vicki near the end of 1999. My younger daughter, Sarah, played matchmaker. Still very fragile after the death of her mother, Sarah, then twenty-six, met Vicki at a party in New York. They fell into conversation about Caroline. As they parted, Sarah asked her, "Can my dad call you?" Sarah phoned me shortly thereafter: "Dad, I met someone who reminded me of Mom. You should call her."

I had started dating about eight months after Caroline's death in 1998. Meeting women wasn't a problem. I was reasonably well known in Boston, a successful physician, trim, athletic, and—false modesty being disingenuous—attractive. (Even my brother once said I had "movie-star" good looks. I *think* he meant it as a compliment.) At Sarah's urging, I picked up the phone and called Vicki.

Our first date almost precluded a second. I took Vicki, worldly, refined, and classy, to a downscale diner with paper napkins and ketchup bottles on the tables, not exactly the place to make a good first impression. But we did go out again, and our relationship quickly blossomed. We were passionate, intense, and sexual. Within months, I was arranging to sell the house in which Caroline and I had raised our daughters, and Vicki and I started looking for a house in which to start our new life together. Four years after the devastating blow of Caroline's death, I was, at last, very much in love again. I basked in the glow of a new beginning and dreamed fairytale dreams about the days ahead. Vicki remembers walking our dogs on a beautiful fall day shortly after our wedding, thinking life could not be more perfect. Then, within weeks of our wedding day, my symptoms started to worsen, the slowness started to descend, and the health episodes that had punctuated our courtship began to appear as interrelated parts of a larger, deeply troubling puzzle.

One of the biggest strains in the first year of our marriage was my insistence that my still-undiagnosed Parkinson's be kept secret. I was in denial and didn't want a word breathed that I was having any kind of difficulty. The Boston medical culture—macho, tough, competitive—inveighed against it. This was an unbearable imposition on Vicki and contrary to how she has always lived her life: tackling problems head-on and with candor. The stress was enormous, especially as my condition worsened and the drama unfolded at the office. Desperately in need of answers but not wanting to betray my trust, where could she turn?

* * *

When we decided to marry, Vicki's intention was to take a year off after our wedding; a year away from her busy practice and the demands of clients; a year with far less responsibility than she had been shouldering; a year to imagine the possibilities that our new marriage had to offer. Instead, she now has more responsibility than ever. I am a burden, and I know it.

Though I still drive, very deliberately, to a few nearby places— Peet's for my coffee, my office (I still maintain an office at the Lown Center), and to spin class—I can't simply hop in my car and go off to Fenway Park, to shop, or to visit friends. Spontaneity is no longer a part of my life. Vicki, too, has lost her independence, though she is perfectly able of mind and body: She is tethered to me, and I to her. My limitations have imposed a parallel set of limitations on her. She can't travel without making some arrangements for me at home, and she worries about me while she is away. When we do travel together, she has to prepare for the trip differently than she would have if I had been well. Everything has to be structured around my limitations.

Though she shoulders the enormous burdens of caretaking with seeming aplomb, I know there are times when it seems more than she can bear, that she wishes she had more time alone (with me, presumably, busy with my medical practice), that she had the independent, self-sufficient husband she expected. What Vicki anticipated our life together would be like couldn't be further from the reality it has become. Had we been married for decades when Parkinson's barged its way into our lives, one might have expected unquestioned loyalty and support from a spouse. For a new wife whose husband kept from her his deepest fears about his health, her loyalty is nothing short of miraculous.

Though Vicki has maintained her interior design career, her real job, she says, is to keep me well. She does it with the same extraordinary competence that she brings to everything. Before Parkinson's, at least before the symptoms became so pronounced, there was only one thing that I was more competent at than she, and that was medicine. From the tennis court and the dance floor to financial planning and running an efficient, orderly household, I never held a candle to her. She is, quite simply, the most capable person I know, and her competence extends to every imaginable part of our lives.

I try to pitch in where I can, but there isn't anything Vicki can't do faster and better. And she's a perfectionist to boot, so it has taken her time to let go and to allow me, for example, to set the table in my own confused way (silverware in the wrong place, napkins askew). And because part of me deeply resents being dependent, and I know Vicki didn't expect or want to become my caretaker, it has taken me a while to accept the fact that there are countless times when asking for her help—tying my shoes, buckling my belt, organizing my papers—is a shortcut through frustration for both of us. To surrender in this way, to put pride aside, means coming to peace with being dependent and accepting help gracefully. Unless you do that, tension will attend every act of kindness.

But every time I make some small concession, every time I accept help with yet another once-simple task, I come face-to-face with the fact that here is yet one more thing I cannot do for myself, one more loss of control over a tiny piece of my life, one more step down the road I don't want to travel. I hate being infantilized, but for the sake of the greater good, for the sake of harmony, I try to yield gratefully.

These are the sacrifices we make for each other to keep life on a more even keel—Vicki letting me do the things I can do, albeit imperfectly, and me being willing to swallow my pride at times by allowing her to take over without recrimination. I do know this, however: My life without her would be terribly, terribly difficult.

Vicki and I also enjoy a luxury that most Parkinson's patients do not: the means to buffer the ordinary demands of daily living with hired help—a full-time housekeeper, a gardener, a part-time bookkeeper, and a part-time cook who shops and prepares meals that we later put in the oven. Perhaps that sounds extravagant, but it reduces the stress on us both and gives us more time and energy to focus on the hard work of sustaining our marriage amid the turmoil inflicted by Parkinson's. I know that most patients struggling with Parkinson's are doing so without the resources we have. This is not something to apologize for, but it is something to acknowledge and appreciate.

* * *

In the summer of 2006, unbeknownst to me until recently, Vicki called my office just to hear the message on my voice-mail, a message I recorded long before the slowness descended, just to hear the voice of the old Tom, the man she thought she had married. She grieves, as I do, the person I used to be.

So I try, often to excess, to express my gratitude and profess my love, which only makes her burden heavier, for it reinforces the unequal distribution of power in our marriage, power she doesn't want and wears uncomfortably. I sometimes call her my angel, but she doesn't want me to hang a halo on her. She feels she can't—and doesn't want to have to—live up to such lofty, unrealistic expectations.

My inability to share equally in the tasks, large and small, of daily living leaves me feeling useless and inadequate at times. I apologize constantly and try to show my appreciation with flowers or a gift of dance lessons. It's how I try to compensate for what I cannot do. And while I often rail against the limitations

Parkinson's imposes on my life, and get impatient and bitter about it, I don't direct my anger at Vicki. I have seen many patients, beleaguered and beset by disease, lash out at the very people, especially loved ones, who, often with great heroism and selflessness, are caring for them. They despise their dependence, are angry with God, and take aim at the closest targets. I always keep that in mind and try never to allow it to happen.

* * *

Layered on top of all of these issues is the impact of Parkinson's on our love life. The bedroom, as I said, is another place where I have lost much to the disease.

Vicki and I are both passionate people; until my symptoms deepened shortly after our wedding, we enjoyed a very intimate, active, and fulfilling sex life. Today, that fire is nearly extinguished, a consequence of a perfect storm of Parkinson's itself, the medications used to treat it, and menopause.

The first time Vicki and I ever danced together, we were at a cowboy bar in Wyoming. She remembers that it was very sensual and appealing to be with someone who could move so gracefully with her. Indeed, it seemed like we'd been partners for years. The rigidity and trembling that are characteristic of Parkinson's have now changed all that. The grace and fluidity of movement that can add so much texture and sensuality to dancing and lovemaking are gone. And it's hard to feel masculine, and sexual, when your wife has to help you cut your food, tie your shoes, and wipe a little drool from your lips. It's hard to see yourself as a sexual being when your partner has to help you off the floor after you fall, pour your juice, or take a Kleenex to your dripping nose.

To cope with this unwelcome change in our life, we have adjusted our expectations and reconsidered the concept of intimacy. Men, and some women as well, tend to focus—far too much, in my view—on how long they can sustain sexual activity and on orgasm. We focus now on simply enjoying our intimate physical contact, regardless of orgasm, and appreciate more deeply the time we have to cuddle, to kiss, to lie side by side, to embrace. We have come to see sensitivity to each other's emotional needs as a form of intimacy. We try to keep things light, and we have our own inside jokes about the state of our sex life that, in themselves, create a feeling of intimacy and privacy. And I always make sure Vicki knows that I still find her sexy and beautiful and desirable.

I have taken a cue from the literary critic Anatole Broyard, who wrote eloquently about living with prostate cancer before succumbing to the disease in 1990. The drugs used to treat the cancer, he was told, would kill his libido. "My libido is no longer lodged in my prostate," wrote Broyard, "but in my imagination, my memory, my conception of myself, my appreciation of women and of life itself. It belongs as much to my identity and my aesthetics as it does to my physiology. When the cancer threatened my sexuality, my mind became immediately erect."

Nevertheless, I do desperately miss the sexuality Parkinson's has stolen from us, and I mourn the loss of my sexuality as I mourn the loss of other parts of me. Like all patients with a serious disease, I hope for a cure; and, short of a cure, I hope for a treatment that will restore me as a complete sexual being.

Just as Parkinson's has cleaved off parts of my intellect like so many icebergs calved from a glacier, it has, in a sense, emasculated me as well.

* * *

Given all the havoc Parkinson's has imposed on our lives, it's not surprising that anger is a major part of the equation in our marriage. The anger that swirls around our marriage is of two kinds.

One is personal: anger directed at someone. As the severity of my illness revealed itself over the first few years of our marriage, as Vicki came to realize that I was not who I had purported to be on our wedding day, and that I had concealed my suspicions about my health, she was intensely angry with me. Understandably she felt betrayed, deceived, and manipulated. It was not clear that our marriage would survive this original sin.

I came into each of my marriages with an unconditional—no ifs, ands, or buts—commitment, first to Caroline and then to Vicki. I was, as the poker players say, "all in." What attracted me to each of them was my sense that they were the kind of people who would make a similar commitment. And in each marriage, I have been confronted with a crisis of mammoth proportions and a stark reality: Caroline was going to die; and Vicki and I, if our marriage could survive, were going to live the rest of our lives with Parkinson's.

I believe our marriage has survived because we have been willing to expend the effort, time, and money to make it work: money and time with therapists—hers, mine, and ours—and effort with each other in long hours of no-holds-barred conversation. Brutal honesty—about our anger, our hurt, our disappointment, our frustration—was necessary for us to get over the emotional hurdles we had to overcome before we could move forward.

The honesty required sometimes meant accepting that painful things had to be said. On a trip I made alone to visit my daughter Penelope and her family in California, we watched a home movie taken at Penelope's graduation from Cornell more than a decade ago. Watching the old Tom in the film—agile, funny, buoyant—was painful and intensely nostalgic. But when I came home, I was eager for Vicki to see it, to show her what I used to be, because she never knew me when I was at my best. You might think it would be a small indulgence for a man mourning his former self. But Vicki was very candid and very direct. "I don't want to live in the past," she said, "and I don't want to be reminded of what I didn't get." Painful? Yes. Honest? Absolutely. But I understand. Trying to recapture my past is like trying to catch the wind in a butterfly net. Without Vicki there to help me cope in the present, I could spend a lot of time in that field chasing the wind with that net.

Age has worked in our favor as we cope with the travails life has thrown at us. We were both in mid-life, with previous marriages and grown children, when we married. With maturity comes a realization that there are always limitations in marriage, that marriage is not a simple or easy proposition, and that commitment and mutual respect are handmaidens to each other.

And what we found, as we plumbed the depth of the well into which we had fallen together, was that we fundamentally had deep respect for each other. We saw the essential goodness in each other. We saw in each other the values we hold most dear. And that is what saved our marriage. We reached down and came to the conclusion that our marriage was sacrosanct and worth whatever mountains we'd have to climb to save it from the ruins of Parkinson's. We accepted that within our marriage there would be room for complaint, and anger, and frustration, all expressed in a kind of emotional safe-room: that is, with the knowledge that above all else, we could express our feelings, no matter how raw, safe in the knowledge that it would not destroy our marriage. We willed it to be so.

Yet despite this commitment, we both remain fragile. For Vicki, this means walking a tightrope, for in some ways I am defenseless. How do you get angry (and I don't mean how *can* you get angry, I mean how *do* you get angry—what *form* do you allow your anger to take) with someone who has dementia and can't necessarily think quickly enough, or clearly enough, to fight back? How do you get angry at someone whose dependence on you is so great that they feel they cannot risk your ire, justified or not?

And for my part, as the dependent party, the one whose original sin saddled Vicki with Parkinson's, can I risk venting my own anger? Do I ever have a right to complain or get angry with Vicki *about anything*? Or is my indebtedness to her so great that I have forfeited that right? Lurking behind these questions is the primal fear of abandonment that has stalked me since the days when my parents subcontracted my early care to a series of nannies. This puts enormous emotional pressure on us both, of course. Vicki must carry the uncomfortable burden of my physical and emotional dependence, and I carry the fear of being alone.

* * *

The second type of anger that marks our marriage is one that we share. I call it situational anger: anger at the circumstances in which we find ourselves. This is an existential anger: at God, at the fates, at being on the short end of the stick. It's harder to put such anger to rest, to find closure, because there is no one to blame, no one on whom we can focus our discontent, no one to apologize to us for the harm and hurt they have caused, and no one to reconcile with.

As Vicki has asked many times, "Why is this happening to us?" There is, maddeningly, no answer to that question; one can only strive to accept, not to know. There has been no closure, and I suspect there never will be, to our existential anger. It is pervasive, it is deep, and it is with us day in and day out. We manage it, but I doubt we will ever conquer it.

* * *

There is one all-important question above all others hanging over our marriage like a storm cloud that won't budge: What will the future bring? My biggest fear is that I will lose even more control over my day-to-day life. I will likely live another twenty years or more, but what will those years be like as the dementia progresses? How quickly will it progress? Will I lose it completely, or will I retain enough of myself to make life worth living? And what will the progression mean for the quality of

Vicki's life? Will she be caught in that awful twilight zone that the loved ones of Alzheimer's patients so often inhabit, caring for the shell of a person held dear?

After my diagnosis and the realization that I was in the early stages of dementia, I used to reread my CV to bolster my sagging self-esteem. Today I am more accepting of the person that I have become, even if I am bitter and angry about it. My self-esteem, like my central nervous system, has taken a huge hit. Dementia is by far the most difficult of my clinical problems. Today I can still function well enough intellectually to work through the issues in our marriage, participate in major decisions we make as a couple, and provide meaningful companionship.

But what if that changes? If I become increasingly intellectually disheveled, will Vicki still respect my opinions? Will I still be able to provide that meaningful companionship and support? Will I have any credibility with her?

We could be in for a horrendous—and prolonged—ride. Uncertainty is our constant companion. We cope by staying busy and by trying to squeeze all the pleasure we can out of whatever time we have, while hoping that the same hand of fate that gave us Parkinson's will ensure that my condition stabilizes, or at least progresses glacially. We strive for normality, even though it takes considerable effort, and in many cases we fall short.

* * *

This is the complex emotional landscape of our marriage. There is no escaping the fact that Parkinson's has exacted an enormous toll. It infiltrates every aspect of our lives, around the clock, every day. It means we often walk on eggshells and are more deliberate than we would otherwise be about our behavior toward each other. Our marriage is not the fairy tale we imagined, and it never will be. Every day, we bump up against the limitations that Parkinson's has imposed on us. But we are doing it together, not as individuals who simply call themselves husband and wife.

I don't know if one ever fully comes to peace with circumstances like these, but I do know that Vicki gives me a reason not to surrender to the despair that anger can breed. There isn't a day that goes by when I don't rail, in some way, at the raw deal we got. But I also know that to give in to that despair would consume enormous amounts of emotional and psychic energy that I need to invest, positively, in my marriage.

I owe it to Vicki to soldier on and live as fully as I am able. I am a husband and father first and foremost, and a Parkinson's patient after that.

Despite the pervasive influence of Parkinson's on our life, I struggle not to let the disease define me, but to live as fully as I can within the limitations imposed by the disease. Parkinson's is like one of those rooms in a horror film where the walls start to close in on you. I don't retreat to the corner and cover my head with my hands and wait for the walls to crush me; to the contrary, I push back and make use of as much space as I still have. Without Vicki, I doubt that I could muster the defiance needed to do this. She doesn't let me feel sorry for myself. She's always looking forward. Even though we both fear where Parkinson's and Lewy body disease may lead us, Vicki has taken my hand for our walk into an uncertain future.

FOUR

Doctors and Patient

FOR MOST OF MY ADULT LIFE I saw myself, first and foremost, as a physician. Over the past few years I have been forced to view myself as a patient. In that regard, I am a work in progress.

It is hardly unique for a physician to become a patient. It happens every day. Doctors, despite their pretensions at times, are human too. But each patient's relationship to his illness is as unique as the individual. Each of us brings to illness all of our life experience and the same complex emotional makeup we bring to every other aspect of our lives. My view of my illness, my behavior with respect to it, and my expectations of my doctors—my neurologist, Dr. John Growdon, and my psychotherapist, Dr. Susan Block—are all shaped, in part, by my own experience as a physician.

In other words, Parkinson's may not be unique to me, but I am unique to my Parkinson's. I am not a collection of symptoms to be managed; I am a complex person, and I want caring physicians who see all of me and who are willing to walk down the path of Parkinson's with me. In my neurologist, of course, I want a doctor who understands Parkinson's inside and out, but I want him to understand me inside and out too. In my psychotherapist, I want someone who doesn't just listen to my problems; I want someone willing to struggle with me for answers, to provide comfort, and to help me adjust to the ever-changing reality of my life as Parkinson's chips away at my mind and body.

* * *

If an illness or injury isn't life-threatening or has a definitive cure, most of us would be satisfied to find a physician with the technical skills to set us right. We might prefer that he or she had a refined bedside manner, took our anxieties and fears to heart, and greeted us with warmth and kindness, but mostly we'd just want to get the job done right. It would be nice if he was a *mensch,* but we don't need the orthopedic surgeon replacing our knee to be a poet.

However, the patient with a chronic or life-threatening illness, or one that dramatically alters quality of life such as Parkinson's, deserves more, needs more, and yearns for more from his doctor. Such patients and their families are inevitably in an existential and spiritual crisis, not just a medical one. And while the doctor is not a clergyman, for a patient in crisis it helps if the doctor is something of a philosopher—and it helps the physician too. Impoverished is the doctor who deals every day with life and death with nothing more than a cold clinical efficiency.

"I see no reason or need for my doctor to love me—nor would I expect him to suffer with me," wrote Anatole Broyard when he was dying of prostate cancer. "I wouldn't demand a lot of my doctor's time; I just wish he would *brood* on my situation for perhaps five minutes, that he would give me his whole mind just once, be bonded with me for a brief space, survey my soul as well as my flesh, to get at my illness, for each man is ill in his own way."

I tried to be the kind of doctor that Broyard longed for; and now, living in the twilight zone of Parkinson's, I look for a bit of myself in my doctors.

* * *

Dr. Y was a sixty-two-year-old physician from New Jersey when he came to me more than a decade ago for a second opinion, after being urged by his cardiologist to have either a stent implanted or coronary bypass surgery. His case was typical of many I saw during my years in practice.

After a standard exercise test, Dr. Y had been told that he was at risk for a catastrophic heart attack, even though he felt well and had no symptoms. He did, however, present with several risk factors for coronary disease: He was a smoker, and he had elevated cholesterol and mild hypertension. His wife was battling breast cancer, which weighed heavily on him. He was told to curtail virtually all activities, lest he do something to precipitate a heart attack.

By the time he came to me, Dr. Y was, understandably, in a state of high anxiety about his heart. He'd been told, as so many heart patients are, that he had "a time bomb in his chest," words that only exacerbate the stress that is often a major factor in heart attacks.

The most important step in cases like this, before further testing, is to give the patient ample opportunity, in an unhurried setting, to voice their anxieties, to decompress, and to unburden themselves of their fear.

After taking a detailed history, Dr. Y and I talked for a while before I asked him to take a second exercise test in our office, a test that confirmed the presence of coronary disease (a narrowing of major vessels). But there was good news on examination, too: Dr. Y's heart rhythm and heart muscle function were normal. Since he had no symptoms—no chest pain, no shortness of breath—and all of his major risk factors could be modified, there was every reason to be optimistic about his prognosis without surgical intervention. His high cholesterol and mild hypertension were both treatable with medications and exercise. And now that he had a strong motivation to do so, he could also, with support, quit smoking.

This was fifteen years ago, and Dr. Y is still alive and well. He had no cardiac surgery, and the "time bomb" in his chest is working fine. Dr. Y is doing well, in part, because I listened to his voice, not just his heart, and because the optimism I conveyed made a believer of him as well.

In such cases, it is important to get "buy-in" from a patient's primary care doctor. Another patient of mine, a Dr. Z, also from New Jersey, also did fine with a similar management approach, but every year after his annual visit, during which I would allay his anxiety about his mild and treatable heart disease, his primary care physician would ratchet up the anxiety by introducing an element of doubt about my conservative, non-interventional approach. By projecting his own anxiety onto the patient, this doctor was undoing, inadvertently, much of what I was trying to accomplish—keeping Dr. Z's anxiety, itself a risk factor, in check.

In both of these cases, exorcising anxiety and reducing stress is an essential part of an overall management strategy that combines medications and risk factor modification. To be successful, the doctor has to convey conviction—while also projecting assurance—that the patient, if he follows the management plan, will do well. This, in turn, requires an approach to patients that bucks current trends in medicine in which economics drives the train and limits the amount of time (the doctor's most precious commodity) a doctor can spend with a patient. But the doctor's time is also a precious commodity *for the patient;* and to forge the trust needed for a successful partnership, the physician must be able to give generously of his time. If you let the patient speak unhurriedly, he will often tell you something essential to the diagnosis, and your willingness to listen to at least part of his life story signals your concern for the individual, not just his heart muscle.

Among the many questions I asked my patients, I *always* asked two that seemed disarmingly simple, but which often gave me a window into their lives: Do you look forward to going to work in the morning? And, do you look forward to going home at night? I would tell patients not to rush, but to really think about the questions and their answers before responding. Not only did the questions signal my interest in them as individuals, but the answers often revealed much about the stress on their hearts and clues about how best to manage their heart disease.

* * *

A few days before a regular six-month appointment with my neurologist, John Growdon, in late 2006, I was asked what, if anything, I would like him to do for me that he wasn't doing already. My answer was quick and sarcastic: "I'd like him to call me every month to ask how I'm feeling," I snapped, as if a busy doctor with hundreds of patients in his care would have time for *that*.

But the more I thought about it, the more I realized that my glib remark cut close to the truth. I want to be on his radar screen. I want him to be thinking about my case, not just when

I am in his office, but when he reads about new treatments and new insights into Parkinson's and Lewy body dementia. I want him to be turning my case over in his head once in a while, and I want to know that while there is nothing that exists today to reverse my dementia, he is thinking from time to time about how to make my life better.

When I saw Growdon a few days later, I asked if we could increase the frequency of our regular consultations from every six months to every three months, to which he readily agreed. Why? For the simple reason that the Parkinson's path is taking me through very unfamiliar and forbidding territory. I want a guide—someone I trust who knows the medical terrain, someone who has been down the path with others—to be there in spirit and in mind. I want someone mindful of the pitfalls, the traps, and the forks in the road. It may well be that little will change in my clinical condition over three-month intervals, but I don't want to see Growdon every three months merely to size up incremental changes in my symptoms or to tweak my medications; I also want the comfort of his presence and to know that every once in a while we can, in Broyard's words, brood over my situation together.

In my own practice, I developed a keen sense of just how deeply appreciated and how profoundly comforting small acts of kindness and mindfulness can be for the patient and his or her family. Dropping in on a hospitalized patient at the end of a busy day, not to check the chart or to do a quick exam, but just to say, "Hello, I just came by to see how you are. Is there anything you need?" Calling a patient at home a few weeks after their annual visit to see how their new diet and exercise program is progressing. Writing a letter of condolence to the family of a patient who has died (a sorely neglected necessity, in my view). These small acts say to the patient and the family, "I know you ache, I know you suffer, I know you are in pain," and allows doctor and patient to meet on the common ground of their mutual humanity.

I am not a surgeon, but when a patient of mine was scheduled for surgery, cardiac or otherwise, I always tried to pay a social visit in the hospital the night before, or tried calling them at home if they weren't yet hospitalized. I can't prove it, of course, but I believe such a visit or call decreases operative mortality. Such social calls were invariably welcomed and comforting. There is no way to measure the curative and healing power of such a bond between doctor and patient, but I am utterly convinced of its salutary effect.

It is also hard to overstate the importance of the doctor's literal laying-on of hands. Years ago I had a patient, Mrs. H, who had been hospitalized with terminal gastric cancer. It was her cancer, not her heart disease, that was threatening her life; but every day, as I rounded with my medical students and stopped to examine Mrs. H, I routinely listened to her heart. One day, under pressure of time, I forgot; and as I turned to leave, she said, "Dr. Graboys, aren't you going to listen to my heart?" I was embarrassed and flustered in front of my charges and immediately struck by the fact that although she knew her heart was not her major problem, she needed and wanted the reassurance of my touch.

As I reflected on the experience later, I also realized that Mrs. H. had interpreted my actions as a commentary on her condition. My failing to listen to her heart that day signaled a loss of hope in her situation. If I could no longer be bothered to examine her heart, it meant the cancer was so serious that it had rendered her heart problem irrelevant. Conversely, by examining her heart, I had been signaling hope that she was not succumbing to her cancer.

Similarly, a doctor's words—as my mentor, Bernard Lown, has written—can maim or they can heal. The physician who offers nothing more than impeccable clinical judgment can, nevertheless, draw the cloak of illness tight around a patient with carelessly chosen words. Too many times, patients have come to me and said that another cardiologist described their heart as a "widow-maker" or a "time bomb." The stress and anxiety thus induced by the doctor can turn him into a prophet. Words that allay stress, words that allow room for hope—not false hope, but hope—can allow the patient to shift the burden of worry onto the physician.

So I know what I look for in a doctor.

* * *

My first meeting with Growdon in 2004 was permeated by my acute stress. I was there because something momentous was happening within and I feared it. And stress exacerbates all of my symptoms. So there I sat, sweating profusely, my mind a jumble, unable to articulate a coherent thought. Growdon opened the conversation simply: "How can I help you?" These seemingly innocuous words, too, are significant. Importantly, he did not begin with a negative: "So, what's wrong?" but with words that signaled his purpose: to help. I appreciated that.

Vicki had to speak for me and provide the medical history that had led me to Growdon's door. I don't know what his first impression was of the dysfunctional human being sitting before him, but our first impression was that Growdon was kind and decent and empathetic.

From the time I had my first episode of near-syncope in London in 2002, not long before the Bermuda episode that resulted in my receiving the pacemaker, to the time I first saw Growdon, I had been acting as my own primary care physician. I was in the "maybe it will all go away" magical-thinking phase of my illness. As a long-practicing physician used to being in control of other people's health, I trusted myself more than anyone else to take care of my own. But something insidious was at work. A serious health problem had implications that I was not prepared to accept, so I maneuvered to ensure that I didn't get bad news: I took control of the flow of my own medical testing, thus depriving myself of an objective medical assessment of my condition.

In truth, to say I "managed my own care" and "took control of the flow of my own medical testing" is a fancy way of saying that I did nothing to address the growing problem. In fact, I avoided medical testing, and I became curt and irritable with anyone who inquired about my health. Overconfident and arrogant, I was, in retrospect, a terrible doctor to myself and could no more conceal my increasing symptoms than I could conceal my face; and that was part of the problem—the illness was already etching itself into my physical appearance. When my friends John Rutherford and Gilbert Mudge, both physicians, expressed their concerns to Vicki, concerns that she then shared with me, I called both of them and told them, angrily, that they should come to me directly, not to my wife, and then insisted that nothing at all was wrong. I was wounded, but mostly I was fortifying my wall of denial.

I was looking for a way out, for a way to avoid all the implications a serious illness would have for my life. But by playing doctor to myself, I simply interfered with a timely diagnosis and treatment. The delay made life for Vicki, for me, and for those around me much more difficult, for my increasingly problematic symptoms were going untreated. Looking back, I have to admit that my behavior was astonishing, outrageous, and foolish, an unfortunate testament to the strength of my defense mechanisms when confronted with the unthinkable.

* * *

I was still working, struggling to carry a full workload, when I came under Growdon's care, and would, as I have described, fight desperately to continue my clinical practice for another year.

When I first consulted Growdon, I didn't want my as-yet undiagnosed condition to be public. Because so many in Boston's medical community knew me, I wanted everything about my case to be kept private. I didn't want information available to anyone with access to the computer system at Mass General, where Growdon works. I didn't want my physical file available to staff at the Movement Disorders Clinic, which he directs. I didn't even want to be seen in the clinic's waiting room, because I didn't want whispers going around that I was consulting a specialist in neuro-degenerative disease. I still thought, unrealistically, that if they didn't know, no one would notice that anything was wrong.

Growdon was sensitive to my need for privacy and has continued to see us, as he did at the beginning, in his private office. He has placed my medical records beyond ordinary reach. It is one of the perks of having been a member of the medical club. But it also signaled to me that Growdon was willing to meet me on my own terms: that he understood the far-reaching implications of my own particular struggle.

There was something else that endeared him to me. He assumed the posture of an advocate—*my* advocate. He wasn't going to vouch for my ability to continue to practice medicine if he didn't believe that to be the case; but he was going to be my partner in doing everything we could, particularly pharmacologically, to enable me to work. He took the most optimistic view possible under the circumstances. When I needed someone to take up the battle with me, Growdon, deliberately and carefully, helped me to do everything that could be done to salvage my career. That the battle would eventually be lost was inevitable, looking at it in retrospect, but his posture of advocacy was not. And today, though we are farther down the Parkinson's road, Growdon is still an advocate for my living life as fully as I can.

Sometimes his advocacy is subtle. Patients, and I count myself among them, are often psychologically fragile. And for me, the issue of driving an automobile has come to assume enormous symbolic and psychological importance. As my world has constricted, as I have become more and more dependent on Vicki and others to help me with many of the simple tasks of daily living,

I cling to my limited ability to drive to the few places I can still go as the last vestige of independence I have. A few years ago, I could travel anywhere, any time. Today, even my daily trip to the coffee shop requires that I replay the route in my mind and that I concentrate intensely on my driving. But that trip to the coffee shop, or the occasional drive to the office, is the limit of my unassisted mobility in the world. To lose this small remnant of independence would be psychologically catastrophic.

But should I be driving, even the mile to the coffee shop? It's a question that dogs me every time I make the trip. I no longer hop in the car without worry. Every short trip is fraught with anxiety. Am I a danger to others? To myself? Given how desperate I am to continue to drive, can I ever be honest enough with myself to call it quits before it's too late? And yet, despite being weighted with all this stress, that little drive means everything to me.

Not long ago, during one of my excursions, I was involved in a minor accident: A woman driving around a corner in a parking lot hit my car. She apologized profusely and promptly sent a check to cover the damage, preferring not to contact her insurance company. But, at the moment of impact, my first thought wasn't: Is she okay? Am I okay? No, it was: How am I going to convince Vicki that the accident had nothing to do with my Parkinson's? Though I drive much more cautiously with the Parkinson's, I do have a propensity to hit the curb now and then. So Vicki is ever-vigilant about my driving, and I feared that this minor accident might be the death knell of my solo trips for coffee.

When Vicki and I put the driving question to Growdon, I was struck by the sensitivity of his response. He said nothing at first, but his eyes betrayed an understanding of how desperately I want to hold on to my car keys, and what a powerfully loaded issue driving is to me. The safe and easy answer for him, the least morally ambiguous, would have been "no." He knows I can afford to take a cab. He listened to me describe the limited driving I do, and without mandating any particular course of action he then said, "Let's see what we can do that will allow you to drive safely to and from the few nearby places you need to go."

I am never going to hop in a red Mustang convertible with black upholstery like the one I owned in college and head out West, though I have vivid and frequent fantasies of bolting from Parkinson's in that Mustang, music on the radio and Vicki in the passenger seat beside me. But right now, that trip to Peet's coffee shop is my road trip down Route 66, my own *Easy Rider* moment, though nothing about it is easy.

For not taking the easy road himself, for not taking away that one small remnant of independence and freedom of movement, for not playing it absolutely safe, for leaving some room for me to come to my own judgments, I am grateful to Growdon. If he believed my limited driving posed a danger, he would have said so. But because he listened carefully, he knew where I go, how often, and how aware I am of the need for vigilance and caution. So, when I speak of advocating for the patient, it can sometimes mean simply understanding each patient on his own terms and eschewing the easy, pat, overly cautious answers that can make a patient feel that the doctor is responding only to the disease and not the patient.

* * *

Just a few weeks after these words were written, I had another accident, this one more serious. It was dark, and I was at a stoplight less than a mile from home. I'm not sure how it happened, but I collided with a cyclist as I slowly began to move forward when the light changed. He was fine, a few bruises and a damaged bike; but I was, naturally, very upset. The accident might well have happened regardless of the Parkinson's—he wasn't wearing reflective clothing and it was dark. But once again I had to re-evaluate whether I should be driving and, if so, under what conditions. I was rarely driving at night anyway, so the next small step was to eliminate all but daylight driving, another in the endless series of incremental concessions I have had to make to my disease.

* * *

I empathize with the dilemma that Growdon faces with patients like me. In cardiology there are, more often than not, options that can, at the very least, arrest progression of disease or enable patients with heart disease to lead normal lives. In ninety percent of my cases, I could legitimately offer hope and help effect a wholesome outcome. In cardiology we can often determine who is at high risk of a life-threatening event and who is not, and thus provide comfort to a great many patients who come to us in a state of high anxiety.

The physician treating patients with progressive neurodegenerative diseases doesn't have that luxury. Dementia does not go into remission, though it may plateau. Hope is hard to come by. You cannot honestly put a positive face on Lewy body disease. The best news that can be offered is that the rate of decline may be slow; in the end, that isn't terribly comforting.

For physicians who treat patients with incurable life-altering disease, or patients with terminal disease, it is difficult to share the emotional burden of illness. It is hard enough to give yourself over emotionally to one dying human being (whether they are dying physically or mentally). How do you give yourself over to hundreds and still function as a physician, a spouse, and a parent? Some emotional distance is the only way physicians who deal day in and day out with patients like me can function. All day, every day, Growdon is attending to patients and their families in the throes of very complicated illness. And every patient and every family member is needy in some way; their lives, it may well seem to them, hang on his words. Each of them needs his attention, his understanding, and his patience. Each of them wants their case to be his most important.

That is why, as Broyard says, we cannot expect our physicians to suffer with us. But we can expect them to move out from behind the technology and the pharmacology to connect with us briefly, to genuinely share, for a moment, our pain and anguish. I am well aware of the tremendous toll it takes, emotionally, intellectually, and physically, to manage complex cases like mine, let alone hundreds of them year after year, decade after decade. So I don't expect Growdon to brood for long on my condition. He cannot offer a light at the end of the tunnel. What matters is that he is patient, caring, and sympathetic and supports my proactive approach to my life. And, importantly, he never seems rushed, never gives me the sense when we are together that he has anything else to do but attend to me. He is very much *present* in our meetings. He conveys a willingness always to search for ways that will allow me to do as well as I possibly can within the boundaries drawn by Parkinson's.

* * *

There is something to be said in defense of the canard that doctors make lousy patients. We know too much for our own good—but, since most of us specialize, not necessarily enough about our own conditions. It can be a recipe for disaster.

I am not, I am sure, Growdon's easiest patient, because I have not always been a particularly compliant patient. I still have a tendency, though not as pronounced as it was, to try to control my own management. After the disaster a couple of years ago when I took myself off Zoloft because it was depressing my sex life, I have tinkered less with my meds, but I still take it upon myself to tweak them occasionally. Sometimes I have increased them, very slightly, when I feel I am slipping. I have delayed the further cognitive testing Growdon has recommended, because I fear it will show signs of progression.

All of this creates a serious challenge. How can Growdon assess the efficacy of my medications when he can't be sure how much I am taking? How can he best help me when I want him to know that I feel I am deteriorating, but resist testing for fear of what it will show? And unless the results are going to change the management of the disease, I am not interested in measuring how much of my mind I've lost. What am I going to do with that information? Unless it can affect the outcome, there is something to be said for not exhausting every avenue of information about your condition.

Before our most recent meeting, I promised myself that I would not evade how I am feeling or hold back from an honest assessment of how I am doing. I completed the Unified Parkinson's Disease Rating Scale, a self-assessment of my symptoms. Yet, in more than a half dozen measures of motor control, where I recorded very minor impairment, Growdon observed significantly greater impairment. Maybe that's why I put on a jacket and tie for the appointment—to put on a good appearance, in the hopes that he wouldn't see the disheveled, disordered person beneath the crisp dress. I still think, at times, I can outwit my Parkinson's, or at least conceal it, another example of magical thinking.

And there is this: I am arrogant enough to think that I was so good at tending to the emotional needs of patients, and have so much faith in the quality of care I provided as a doctor, that I am distrustful of doctors until they show me that they are smarter and better able to manage me than I am. It's a narcissistic brew of hubris, overconfidence, and self-indulgence. I will be the "wonder doctor" to myself, my very own "dream team." This doesn't make me an easy patient, and I should know—I've had some difficult patients myself.

A few times a year over the course of my practice, I "fired" patients—in a gentle fashion—for chronic noncompliance with plans I had established to protect their well-being. The "firing" would take the form of a suggestion that the patient fire me because I was unable to be sufficiently persuasive with them.

"I think you might do better in the care of another physician," I would say, "because you haven't adhered to our plan. Perhaps another doctor would be more effective." This would usually be met with pleas for another chance and promises to do better in the future, and, indeed, that's often what happened.

One of the most common forms of noncompliance was a patient manipulating his own medications or failing to take them altogether. So here I was, doing precisely what some of my "worst" patients used to do because, I reasoned, I am a brilliant doctor myself; this is within my power, within my expertise, and I feel a sense of control doing it. I can be the master of my own fate. In truth, if I were so brilliant, I wouldn't have myself as my doctor.

It may seem contradictory—because adjusting one's own medications is inadvisable—but I am also, in many ways, a cautious patient. As a cardiologist, I was deeply sensitized to potentially dangerous drug interactions; and my early experience under Growdon's care, when we tried to find an effective combination to alleviate my symptoms, was a perfect example of how drug cocktails that work well in most patients can have debilitating side effects in others. In the earlier stages, I could justify the risks of manipulating my own medications, especially when the cure seemed worse than the disease. As my Parkinson's has progressed, however, the risk-benefit ratio has shifted. Early on, I thought, "What I don't take can't hurt me"; now I am more prepared to accept the risks that come with medication, more willing to adhere to the plan Growdon has laid out, because my symptoms are worse.

Am I a good patient? A bad patient? Such language doesn't appear to be part of Growdon's vocabulary. I suspect he would say I am an anxious patient with a strong support system. He acknowledges all that I do to keep going and to keep myself active within the confines of Parkinson's—regular exercise, drum lessons, an active social life. It's how I push back at Parkinson's. That I am proactive in searching for ways to make the most of my life, and perhaps to better my outcome, would, I suspect make me a "good" patient in some respects.

This book is the most dramatic evidence of this push-back. It has given me a reason to get up and "go to work" every day. Despite my diminished intellectual firepower, the process validates my intellect. The day we received an offer from the publisher of this book was one of the best, most hopeful, and most exalted days I have had in years, because it constituted recognition that I still have something important to contribute.

More importantly, the process of writing this book has helped me explain my illness to myself, helped me make sense of my disordered life, given me insights and understanding about the process of being ill, clarified in my own mind the chronology of my illness, and given me a narrative of my illness that somehow helps contain what would otherwise be a riot of emotional upheaval caused by the Parkinson's. It helps me organize the clutter of Parkinson's into a package I can understand. It is, therefore, intensely therapeutic, and Growdon has been a cheerleader of this effort. He knows it is helping me live as fully as I can; and that, I think, makes me a "good" patient, too. I am taking as much control as I can over a life in which losing control is *the* central theme, *the* defining characteristic.

* * *

My primary ally in the struggle to make order out of disorder, to adjust to the new realities of my life, and to cope with the depression, fear, and anger that are part and parcel of my illness, is my psychotherapist, Dr. Susan Block. (Because I call her Susan in person, I will do so here.) On a week-to-week basis, Susan is the physician most intimately involved in my care, and she is everything I could hope for in a doctor.

If it is too much to expect our internists, cardiologists, and neurologists to give themselves over unsparingly to our emotional and spiritual needs, it is the therapist's raison d'être to toil in that vineyard. But not every therapist is capable of making a deep, personal, emotional connection with patients. Susan is especially well qualified to understand the emotional landscape of the seriously ill; she works primarily with terminally ill patients as chief of the Division of Psychosocial Oncology and Palliative Care at Boston's renowned Dana Farber Cancer Institute. As codirector of Harvard Medical School's Center for Palliative Care, she recruited me into a program that pairs terminally ill patients, and others with chronic life-altering illnesses, with first-year Harvard medical students. The program aims to teach soon-to-be physicians the importance of listening and compassion in the care of the seriously ill, and to attune them to the spiritual and emotional needs of patients. Susan thought the students could learn from me because, as a physician and medical educator, I always tried to embody this approach. But she also thought the program would be therapeutic—a way for me to remain engaged in shaping the sensibilities of the next generation of doctors.

* * *

I first met Susan when Caroline was dying of cancer. She helped all of us—Caroline, the girls, and me—through the worst crisis in our lives, at times coming to our home in the final days of Caroline's life. She has been privy to the most intimate details of my life ever since, and now she is navigating the emotional turmoil of Parkinson's and dementia with me.

It was, she says, a "lucky accident" that I already had a long-term therapeutic relationship with her when I became ill, because she already had a wealth of information about the anxieties, fears, and other traits of personality that I bring to my disease. This continuity means that Susan can bring all of her intimate knowledge of the old, pre-Parkinson's Tom to bear in treating the new Tom.

Nowhere is this clearer, or more significant, than in helping me cope with loss. Long before Parkinson's, loss and bereavement were frequent visitors in my life. Growing up, my parents entrusted my care to a series of older women, nannies, to whom I became deeply attached only to see them eventually exit my life, leaving me bereft. Those departures laid the groundwork for a lifetime of anxiety and fear of abandonment. And, of course, Caroline's death, which remains an ongoing source of sorrow, was that prophecy fulfilled. When I speak with Susan about the progressive losses I am suffering with Parkinson's, she knows that my emotional response to them is shaped by these earlier experiences. Therapy at this point in my life is more about coping than feeling better; and being able to see my grief, anger, and despair at being ill in the larger context of my life helps me manage those responses and keep them from consuming me.

* * *

Susan *does*, to use Broyard's word again, brood over my situation, and this allows her to fashion helpful strategies for coping with the challenges I face. Her sensitivity to my fragility over the question of retirement, for example, was both acute and astute. As she was slowly but inexorably moving me to see that retirement was inevitable, she suggested that I make a list of all the things I would want to do if I were liberated from the crushing burdens of work. She saw the toll my masquerade was taking, and this was her way of helping me see that life could and would go on after retirement, even with Parkinson's—that indeed there was a life beyond Parkinson's, beyond medical practice, to be lived at all.

By serving as the repository of the enormous anger I feel about what is happening to me and to those around me, Susan has also helped me to live, with more dignity, with a most undignified disease, and to make as healthy an adjustment as I can to the ever-changing realities of my life. The intense anger has ebbed somewhat over the past three or four years as I have come, grudgingly, to acceptance of the reality of my life.

But anger still accompanies the humiliating moments I suffer in my daily living. The struggle to put a lid on my coffee, to buckle a seat belt, to button a shirt or tie a tie. Each of these is a triviality in isolation, but each a painful reminder of everything that has gone haywire in my life.

Therapy helps me manage the emotional upheaval that comes with this loss of control. By depositing all my anger, pain, and frustration with Susan, it becomes less of a burden at home. Vicki already has too much to contend with, including her own anger, pain, and frustration. The caretaker's role is emotionally and physically demanding, and it is endless. There is only so much one person can bear. Without Susan, I doubt my marriage would have survived my illness.

* * *

Today, some of my most acute moments of psychic pain come when I see former patients or old friends. "You look so good, Tom," is the common refrain. "How are you?" On the phone it's often, "You sound great!" "Thank you," I say, "I'm doing well." I understand that people want to be encouraging. They mean well. But they are also trying to reassure themselves that the doctor or friend they grieve for really is okay. He looks good, so he must be coping well with his Parkinson's. They are relieving their own anxiety about me and about illness.

Though I deeply appreciate the concern of others and don't want people to stop asking me how I'm doing, I confess that there are times when it becomes oppressive. It is impossible for people to understand what my life has become, nor do they necessarily want to know. There are times when that refrain "You look so good" makes me want to bring my fist down on the table and shout, "Please! Acknowledge my illness, understand that beneath this benign exterior I am in turmoil, my world is chaos, and I hurt. I know you need to hear I am okay, but I'm not."

With Susan's help, I am able to bring these feelings into the open and, by so doing, keep them from tearing at me.

Susan doesn't just try to put out the emotional fires, however; she takes a long-term view that focuses on how to conduct one's life with grace and dignity through chronic illness. For example, she has helped me overcome the shame and embarrassment of illness simply by encouraging me to accept its reality. The denial that was so much a part of the early years of my Parkinson's was shaped by my need to maintain the construct of the fairytale life that had started to crumble with Caroline's death. I was proud that I looked twenty years younger than I was, that I was held in high esteem by my patients and the Boston medical community, that I was a good athlete and musician. Parkinson's ripped the face off of all that. That I have come from staunch denial to the point where I am now willing to write this story is a testament to Susan's ability to help me come to terms with my life as it is, not as I might wish it to be.

Susan has said that chronically ill patients seek to explain their illness to themselves, to make sense of what is happening to them, and that the process of putting words to the experience of illness can be very therapeutic. Because my ability to articulate has been so compromised by Parkinson's, and my thoughts are so jumbled, this is especially challenging. But writing this book, which Susan, like Growdon, encouraged, has indeed been intensely therapeutic. As I seek to explain myself, my illness, and my life to others, I explain it to myself. "Much of therapy," Susan has said, "is reflecting and putting words to experience." For me, now struggling to find ordinary words and speak coherent sentences through my dementia, this is especially difficult, but also especially important.

Susan also encouraged this book for another reason, however. She tries always to remind me of my strengths and of the ways I can continue to contribute—to my family and to the community at large. She understood that I did not want to be done with doctoring or with my life's work. One of the most terrible aspects of chronic illness is the feeling of diminishment that accompanies it. Contributing, in ways large and small, can be a counterweight to such feelings. This book has helped restore some, but by no means all, of the "sense of wholeness," as Susan describes it, stolen by illness.

* * *

With Susan, I also continue to explore my continuing relationship with Caroline. It is to Vicki's everlasting credit, and a tribute to her strong sense of self, that she knows and accepts that my grieving for Caroline is a lifelong process. Being seriously, chronically ill has deepened my already-strong spiritual connection to Caroline. In the years immediately after her death, I would often have conversations with her, typically while out running, in which I would speak to her out loud. Today, my "conversations" with her have more of a quality of communion about them. I sit quietly and picture her, usually as she was in the moments immediately after she died, at home, with the four of us, Penelope, Sarah, Caroline, and I, in bed together. Arrangements had been made for members of Caroline's women's group to wash her and cover her in a white shroud she had chosen. When they finished, I came back into her room. Caroline, who had been warm moments before, now felt cold as I kissed her. I sat there, alone with her, for perhaps half an hour. And that is how I usually picture her today.

I often told family members of patients who had died that access to memories of those we have lost can be a source of solace, and so it has been for me. My memories of Caroline—both in death and in the many, many good times of our life—help allay anxiety and provide comfort. Susan has suggested that I feel Caroline's hand guiding me through my illness, and that seems right. I do wish she were here now to help me through my Parkinson's—and perhaps, in a way, she is.

* * *

Because Parkinson's never goes away, there will be no emotional closure—I expect that the anger, frustration, and despair will be with me the rest of my life. They are legitimate responses to the reality of my life. All Parkinson's patients experience loss, but how they experience it depends on their own personal history with loss. A skilled therapist like Susan can help the patient understand how past experience activates emotional responses in the present. And such understanding, for whatever reason, brings with it a greater ability to cope. Susan's style of gentle, quiet suasion has been as essential to the management of my Parkinson's as my medications. She is, quite simply, *indispensable* to my care.

I don't pretend to tell others how to cope with their Parkinson's or dementia. But I do believe that a therapeutic relationship is essential in the overall management of Parkinson's and dementia because anxiety, fear, depression, and anger are almost always part of the clinical picture; for, in the final analysis, these are not just diseases of the brain, they are maladies of the soul.

FIVE

My Family

SEVERAL YEARS AGO, Mr. B, an elderly man in his nineties, came to see me with his wife, who was well into her eighties. Mr. B had been diagnosed with a serious heart problem for which several medications had been prescribed, and the Bs wanted a second opinion. Mr. B was also suffering from end-stage Parkinson's. He was badly hunched over, he suffered from near-paralysis of his limbs, his nose was constantly runny, and he drooled uncontrollably. The cardiac diagnosis layered on top of the Parkinson's was a heavy blow to the Bs and their five adult daughters.

I have always been careful not to make assumptions about patients based on their physical presentation, because common biases can often interfere with clear-eyed clinical judgments. Indeed, Mr. B illustrated the point well. Though he appeared demented, he was in complete control of his faculties and was still engaged in his real estate and insurance business.

At the end of our first meeting, I suggested to Mr. and Mrs. B that they bring all of their daughters (all happened to live in the Boston area) to their next appointment with me. It was the daughters, in fact, who had initially suggested that their father see me for his heart problem, though none had ever met me. But they had read about my holistic approach and felt that I would listen to their parents' saga with an open mind. I thought that I might learn something of value by meeting with the entire family, and that having them together in my office would be enormously reassuring to their elderly father, a testament to their love and devotion.

Indeed, the meeting with the family did all those things and more. First, it became clear that one of the daughters had emerged as the primary caretaker. She was, therefore, an especially critical ally in helping to ensure compliance with whatever recommendations I might make. Second, the show of family unity was indeed very meaningful to Mr. B. But there was a third important outcome as well. My examination of Mr. B revealed that his heart problem was not serious or life-threatening, as he and his family had been led to believe. This news was enormously therapeutic for all of them, for I was able to lift a huge chunk of anxiety from their shoulders. The Parkinson's, quite advanced and serious in its own right, remained, but their fear of imminent cardiac death was gone. Everyone, including Mr. B, was greatly relieved.

* * *

In my medical practice, I always encouraged patients, especially those with more complicated heart problems, to come to the office with their spouse, their lover, or a close family member. From the moment a patient is joined by others in their struggle with illness, the chances of a favorable outcome are increased. Illness is stressful; and stress, in turn, plays a major role in the onset or progression of many illnesses. The support of family and friends, companionship, the touch of a caring, attentive physician, and the knowledge that you are facing illness as one member of a team all have profound psychological and physiological benefits.

When taking a history, or counseling a patient after testing, I preferred having someone close to the patient join us, *not* simply for the emotional support and reassurance that it provided the patient, but because often that third person would provide vitally important information that affected diagnosis, patient management, and/or treatment. Mr. Smith might tell you everything was fine in his life, but Mrs. Smith might allow that Mr. Smith was acutely distressed over the divorce of his adult daughter. Mrs. Jones might tell you she was taking all of her prescribed medication, but Mr. Jones might take you aside and tell you she wasn't. The doctor can often learn much about a patient's life outside his office, just by observing the interaction of a patient and loved ones inside it. Sometimes a single word, a term of endearment used repeatedly by one spouse when referring to the other, can tell you that the patient enjoys a warm and supportive relationship. Are they affectionate? Do they look at each other? Or does their body language signal a difficult or contentious relationship? This isn't just idle curiosity. A heart patient in a stressful marriage has added risk.

But there was yet another reason for having patients come to their appointments with a significant other, most often a spouse or adult child: Family members are, in their own ways, also afflicted. They, too, are living with the disease and can benefit from the doctor's counsel and from feeling that the doctor is their partner in bearing the burden of ill health. Illness is not just a matter for doctor and patient; it affects immediate and extended family and friends, and how illness plays out in any particular family is as individualized as families themselves—the ages, personalities, and life experiences of every family member will play a role in how a family responds to illness. And how the patient responds to his own illness—how he carries and comports himself through his illness—will significantly impact how it affects others. In short, the patient is in a position to exacerbate or ease the burden that family members must bear.

In my experience, seriously ill patients tend to comport themselves in ways that reflect their healthy selves, their "premorbid" personalities, even though their lives are being turned upside down. Though we all become anxious when we are sick, those predisposed to anxiety will find it difficult to control and will raise the anxiety level of those around them. Those who are kind, gentle, and sensitive will comport themselves with great dignity, be respectful of their caregivers, and remain cognizant of the emotional needs of family. For those who live with great hostility or anger, illness will become yet another platform for their rage. Mrs. S was such a patient.

Mrs. S was only in her early thirties, but she had been my patient for many years. She suffered from a congenital heart defect. She was a tough, no-nonsense woman in a troubled marriage. When she was hospitalized, she vented her anger at the staff, the nurses, and the residents. She yelled obscenities and was belligerent. She excluded family members, including her husband, from her care. When her heart condition worsened, she wanted to be in total control. As she became sicker, she got angrier because she was losing control.

The question for me, as her physician, was how to respond to her anger. How could I help decompress her anxiety and her rage?

What she needed from me was access, time to vent, and hope in an increasingly hopeless situation. In the face of uncertainty or a bad prognosis, there is nothing wrong with hope, and one of the most effective ways for a doctor to convey hope is with his time and attention, even when there is little left to do medically. When patients are near the end and you have exhausted everything in your medical repertoire, they and their families will almost always ask, "Isn't there *anything* else we can do?" The doctor's presence and attentiveness give the patient hope, as does a physical examination. Why? Because in medicine, time is a precious commodity, and the patient will interpret the doctor's absence or brevity as a sign that the doctor believes the game is up. When the doctor abandons the patient, the patient abandons hope. Indeed, hope is a big part of what keeps me going now—hope that the progression of my disease will slow or stop altogether; hope that new treatments will emerge; hope that I will persevere.

A bright and articulate woman, Mrs. S wrote me a number of letters in which she explained that because she had grown up with heart disease, she had always been babied by her protective parents and she refused, as an adult, to be treated like an infant again. She knew quite well that her behavior was an effort to project a sense of control over her increasingly uncontrollable situation. Near the end, she started meditating and imaging, an exercise in which patients, typically cancer patients, try to focus their minds exclusively on the "bad cells" in their body in an effort to exert mind over body to control their disease. It was her last hope, and I encouraged her to do anything that would give her a sense of being in control.

While I came into illness with a very different pre-morbid personality and life experience than Mrs. S, I use her example to remind myself of what I do not want to become in the face of disease. While I am mindful that how I conduct myself through the course of my illness can lighten or increase the burden of my illness on others, the nature of dementia means that my ability to assess and judge my own behavior is compromised. Nor do I have a clear sense of how my behavior, my appearance, and my general comportment are perceived by others. And where once I prided myself on being very perceptive about patients, I don't know if I am reading people correctly any more. So it is hard for me to gauge my interactions with my family, and to know if I am helping to ease, rather than add to, the burdens my illness has placed on them.

* * *

For our fused family (Vicki, me, and our respective children) and my extended family, specifically my brother, George, Parkinson's and dementia are like a huge rock dropped into the middle of a pond. The water is most perturbed at the center, but the impact ripples out to the edges. Though different family members are affected differently, no one has been spared.

My brother, eleven years my senior, has always played a central and positive role in my life. He's very accomplished—the former chairman of Citizens Bank, former Secretary of Education for the State of Rhode Island, a member of the board of trustees of the University of Rhode Island—and one of the most honest, ethical, moral people I have ever known. He is the family patriarch now, not only by dint of seniority but also because of his great wisdom and love for family.

George is also the most competitive person I know—in business and in sports. He is intensely focused and has a startling capacity to ignore—and therefore play through—pain. Still wiry and fit into his seventies, whether it's running a marathon or playing tennis, he competes to win. He is tenacious, unforgiving, and exhausting to play with.

Until Parkinson's eroded my physical abilities, we had a lifelong athletic competition, with the decided edge going to George, whether running, playing tennis (I may have beaten him three times in the thousands of sets we have played), or at one-on-one basketball. For ten years we ran competitively together—the Boston Marathon, the Ocean State Marathon in Rhode Island, and countless other road races. Though we still bat the tennis ball back and forth, there is no competition anymore. He will never suggest that we stop, however, even though my tennis is now horrendous and I sometimes experience near-fainting spells on the court.

Twenty years ago, George's best friend died of a heart attack playing tennis with him, and I suspect it haunts him still. Yet when we play, he will continue until I call it quits. I appreciate that he treats me like an adult, even though I know he's worried sick that something will happen to me, or my pacemaker, on the court. I, in turn, worry that at his age *he's* pushing too hard and that he won't have the "internal sensors" that will tell him it's time to stop.

As my illness emerged, George became increasingly distraught and made sure I understood that he was available at any time for any kind of support he could offer. He was careful not to interfere or to be prescriptive—I always carried the medical portfolio in the family, and I still do. He was very solicitous, always concerned, but never pushy.

But I know he has a high level of anxiety about me. I understand all too well the role of stress on the heart. So it is important, for his sake, that I relieve him of as much anxiety as I can. I try to minimize his risk by not loading his plate with my problems. For someone as accomplished as George and as used to being in control and being able to effect major change, he now finds himself in a situation where he can't control the outcome. I try to gauge each person's threshold for bearing some of the burden of my illness. Protecting George is important to me, because I derive great comfort from having him in my life.

Several months ago, for this book, I asked George to speak as openly as possible about how my illness has affected him.

GEORGE GRABOYS: Tom and I have always been close. I became something of the family patriarch relatively early, because our father took ill when we were young. For example, I became the trustee of the funds for Tom's medical education and, being more than a decade older, I was very much the big brother in almost a parental way.

But after Tom married Caroline and moved back East after serving in the Air Force, we also became very close, not just as siblings, but as best friends. I was always able to take my most personal problems to him, and vice versa. We went to the same prep school and even though we are almost twelve years apart we have always been very similar in many ways, even ordering the same food. Our wives got along well, so we were friendly as couples, too, and spent a lot of time together, traveling, playing tennis, and socializing with each other. Tom and I also ran road races together, pacing each other in several marathons. Later, I got involved in the Lown Cardiovascular Research Foundation (where Tom worked) as a member of the board, so our lives began to intersect professionally, too. And going through Caroline's illness together, and then her death brought us even closer. Tom felt horrible that he couldn't cure Caroline. He was so caring to her when she was sick. He took his marriage vows very much to heart and followed them to the letter. His devotion was extraordinary. Shortly after Caroline died, our sister died, and now we are the only remaining members of our nuclear family. All this has made us very, very tight.

When Tom and Vicki found each other, I thought it was a match made in heaven, and I have great admiration for Vicki and how she has handled this very difficult situation. When he told me he had collapsed when they were in Bermuda, and twice more, that was the first time I was ever concerned about his health. I was right there when he came out of the recovery room after he had the pacemaker implanted. We both thought *that* was the issue and that it had been taken care of.

When I got involved with the Lown Foundation, Tom was taking over from Bernard Lown as chairman. He was the heir apparent to run both the medical practice and the research foundation. But he had no experience administering an organization, and I wanted to coach him a bit about how to run a meeting effectively and how to relate to the board members, because when you assume leadership of an organization, you wear a new cloak. When you are as successful as he had been, you acquire self-confidence, but you may not have the same self-confidence in a new role. At meetings, he started searching for words and he sometimes seemed to lack concentration. I attributed these lapses to his being in a new, unfamiliar role.

I had always been a huge feeder of patients to the Lown Group. I knew a lot of people who, at one time or other, needed a cardiologist; and Tom was so busy, it was hard to get in to see him. I would help people I knew get appointments with him. One day I got a call from one of those people, who asked me if something was wrong with Tom. So it wasn't just his adjusting to his new role at the Foundation, and I started to scrutinize him more closely. I noticed that his tennis wasn't as good as it had been, and he just didn't seem like himself.

I always took great pride in Tom. He attracted people. He was magnetic, funny, quick on his feet, a raconteur, and so articulate even in spontaneous situations. As he thinks about himself now, and about the loss of many of these abilities, he is forced to acknowledge how different he is, and he worries about how people see him.

I despair over what has happened and about what may yet happen. Whatever Tom wants me to do, I will do. I will do *anything* for him. I grieve very deeply for him; the sadness and despair go right down to the core, it's a heavy emotional blow. It's simply heartbreaking for me. I just try and give him as much support in every conceivable way as I can, and I know he'd do the same for me.

As a physician, he was extraordinarily devoted. He took his patients' illnesses to heart, and he grieved for patients who died. He was the health-care giver to our extended family, too. When anyone had a question, we always went to Tom. He had been articulate all his life, and he was a brilliant physician, but now it's very hard for him to reach back for answers that he once could access easily. The last year or so of his practice was especially painful to see, because he couldn't be the doctor he once had been and he struggled so hard to keep going. The pressure he put himself under was so great, and he was losing some of his intellectual edge. I can't bear to think that anyone noticed that he wasn't up to his usual excellence, because he was such a brilliant clinician throughout his career. I don't want to see that legacy tarnished in any way.

The physical changes brought about by Parkinson's— the stooped posture, the mouth agape, the shuffling gait—are also very painful for me to see, as he was always a very graceful athlete.

Tom wants to stay socially integrated, but he feels he has to perform in social situations, which requires tremendous effort and concentration on his part. It's very stressful for him, and the stress seems to worsen his symptoms. Driving is also stressful for him, so I worry a lot about his driving. At the same time, it's so important for his self-esteem that he retain some vestiges of independence. You have to balance the risks, and it's a very difficult calculation. He's at his best when there's no stress, and I try to keep our time together as stress-free as possible.

I can't make sense of how and why this happened. He was on a storybook path, doing something he loved, with a great family, enough money, good looks, and was a giving person in every way; and out of the blue this happens. It's beyond me to explain why. It's just part of the human condition. Asking "why" or "why us" doesn't lead anywhere. The question is: How do we best deal with it? For me, finding ways to sustain Tom's ego and self-esteem, to make sure he has psychic rewards, is very, very important because all the time he's discovering more and more things that he can't do. The book he is writing is a way for him to succeed. He looks for ways to compensate, and so do I; I try to make things easier. If we are hitting the tennis ball and he needs his sneakers tied, which he can't do, I can do that without embarrassing him because we are brothers and friends. It's heartbreaking, though. It means that we are no longer equal parties in a relationship that went so far beyond being siblings. Tom is more dependent now, and the relationship is altered, because he just can't give me the same complex answers to questions that he could before. The relationship has deepened as a consequence of his illness, but obviously in a way that I wish it hadn't.

I am seventy-four and, having lived so long, I have naturally lost family members and close friends. We have a niece who lost two children, for example. I try to accept these losses as fate, but it heightens your sense of vulnerability. As you age and come to grips with your own mortality, you accept more. For whatever reason, this is the hand we have been dealt. We have to play it as compassionately as we can.

* *

My children, Penelope, thirty-six, and Sarah, thirty-three, first met Vicki's children, Jennifer, thirty-two, Carson, thirty, and Olivia, twenty-three, in November 2000. There was the expected awkwardness at first, and ambivalence all around, about where Vicki and I might be heading. Seeing your father with another woman, or your mother with another man, is an adjustment, even for grown children who want nothing more than your happiness. You are checked out, sized up, and judged by your potential stepchildren, and they do the same to one another. It's a bit like buying a house and walking around with a home inspector looking for flaws that might break the deal. But the dinner went well and all the kids left reassured that the others were, in their words, "normal." They liked one another.

It took some time, naturally, for the families to integrate. Indeed, it is still a work in progress. These are adult children, geographically dispersed, so over a series of holidays and vacations they have come to know one another better and have developed relationships that are warm and caring.

For Penelope and Sarah, as my relationship with Vicki deepened, they struggled with feelings about Caroline being displaced. Though she had died a few years before, they were sensitive to any encroachment by Vicki into the space Caroline continues to occupy in our lives. Vicki, to her everlasting credit, has shown extraordinary sensitivity to this boundary without jealousy or resentment. Were that not the case, I don't think our marriage would have survived.

Vicki's children, on the other hand, were simply eager for their mother to have an upstanding man in her life, someone who would be able to take care of her emotionally, someone to go through life with happily and securely. As they got to know me in that brief period before Parkinson's and dementia hit with a vengeance, they grew increasingly comfortable with me—and I with them. I, too, was cautious not to usurp the role of their father, who lives nearby.

Now, as illness has taken center stage in our life, Vicki's kids are back to worrying about their mother, and my children are back to worrying about me. Today, seven years after all our lives intersected, all these innocent souls are caught up in the maelstrom of my illness and are facing complex realities. They have different sets of concerns, and different levels of anxiety and stress, but the pervasive uncertainty that clouds my future and Vicki's is a common burden we all share.

Vicki's children are mature adults, but Carson, more than his sisters, asks questions about Parkinson's, and we have spoken about it on more intimate terms than I have with either Jen or Olivia. But, for the most part, I don't really know what Vicki's children, and to a lesser extent my own, make of what has happened in our lives. Because I am curious to know, I asked each of them, as I did George, to share, with as much candor as possible, how my illness has affected their lives.

Recently married, living in California, and trying to start a new business, my stepdaughter Jen's life is just beginning in many ways. Our trials and tribulations at home are not part of her daily life, but they are taking a toll nevertheless.

JEN BAKER HINTON: When we met Tom, he quickly became our favorite guy of all the men my mom had dated. He was a skier, a tennis player, and very intellectual. He was just a great match for my mom, and we were very excited. Because I understood why my parents divorced, and felt that they were better apart, it wasn't difficult having someone new, especially someone like Tom, in our lives. And, frankly, we were happy to have someone else for my mother to focus on, instead of just us kids.

I was in my mid-twenties when I first met Tom. I wouldn't say we have a deep connection, but I have a loving relationship with him. I live in California, so we just haven't spent enough time together to get to another level.

Everything was great; but when Tom told us he had Parkinson's, it was hard to believe, because his symptoms weren't so noticeable then, at least not to me, and I didn't really understand the ramifications of it or where it would lead. My first thought was "Now what's my mother going to do?" She had created such a good life for herself after the divorce, and when she and Tom married, she and I were both looking forward to there being someone in her life who could take care of her; she'd been taking care of us all these years, and now there'd be someone there to take care of her.

She could see the day when she'd be able to retire—she works so hard—travel, do some volunteer work, and enjoy life. It's very painful to realize that after working so hard, both at her career and at raising her kids, that she won't have the life she wanted and deserved.

She wanted a man to change the lightbulbs and care for her, but my mom has to do all that now. He can't be there for her in many ways, and it hurts both of them. She works very hard to take care of Tom, and it is *a lot* of work.

Life can be such a raw deal. I am very protective of my mother, and I just don't know what the future holds for her. I worry a lot about her and about what will happen down the road. I'm not angry with Tom, but I'm angry about the situation. Tom does the best he possibly can under the circumstances. Sometimes I fantasize that the disease will reverse itself and they'll have the life we all thought they would have together.

It's never occurred to me that my mom should get out of the marriage, but I wish someone could come and help her; however, I can't articulate who and how. My mother and Tom haven't spent a lifetime together, so it seems especially unfair, but you are dealt things in life that aren't fair.

My mom is a natural caretaker—it's in her genes, I think—so maybe there is a reason she was the chosen one. Sometimes, though, it seems like more than she can handle. But she really loves Tom. My mom and I talk about Tom, about the life they are living, about the difficulties. At first she was more emotional about it, but now I think she has it more under control. She needs a support system too, and she has many friends and a therapist—it's important not to struggle with this alone.

Before Tom's illness, I didn't think a lot about mortality. But now I harbor a deep fear that what's happened to Tom could happen to me, or to my husband. I have a much stronger sense now that you have this one chance to live your life, so live it to the fullest because you never know what's around the corner. That's been one of the biggest impacts of Tom's illness on me—a heightened sense of vulnerability.

Tom and I are compatible and friendly, but we haven't really discussed his illness. I would be comfortable talking with him about it, but I'm not sure he'd want to. There have been times when he's apologized for it, which he didn't need to do, but he's very considerate that way—I know he feels awful about the situation and how it affects everyone.

I am recently married and trying to get a business off the ground, and we live three thousand miles away, so I can't say I think about the situation every day. But whenever I talk to my mother, that brings it back into my life.

Having always believed in homeopathic remedies, I sometimes suggest Tom try this or that, but other than that I don't know how I can be of help. I have a hard enough time keeping my own life under control.

I wish they would move out here, though, so we could be closer. One of Tom's daughters is here, and his grandchildren, and he seems to brighten when he's around them. It would add years to their lives to live in San Francisco, being closer to family; and with the weather here, they could live where they could walk everywhere. To me, Tom has seemed pretty much the same for the past couple of years, though I think he seems quieter.

About a year or so ago, we all went to see the Rolling Stones at Fenway Park. Tom was smiling the whole time. He was so into it and having such a great time, just incredibly excited. I was watching him with my mom that night, and they looked like two kids on a date. That's what I wish it were like for them all the time.

* *

Vicki's son, Carson, also lives far away, in California, and is about to be married. Maybe because we are both men, he feels more at ease than his sisters asking me directly about my illness. Like Jen, he worries for his mother, but his sense of powerlessness to affect the situation is also very pronounced and troubling to him.

CARSON BAKER: The real effect of Tom's illness on me is indirect, through my mother. I live far away, so I don't see it close-up day to day. It's conversations with my mother that raise concerns for me.

She finally meets the right guy, and the next thing you know he has this horrible disease and her life isn't anything like she expected it to be. I feel just terrible for my mother, and I constantly worry about how she's doing, how she's holding up under the strain. She has a hard shell and holds the fort. She tackles the challenges head-on without torturing herself with questions like "What if?" or "Why didn't I know?" She accepts that these are the cards she's been dealt.

Like Jen, it pains me to see that she can't have the life she wanted to have, that this disease will consume their lives. Understandably, more of her attention goes to Tom and his family at times. She gives generously of herself, not just to him, but to Penelope and Sarah too. My mom's concern with Tom and the physical and emotional energy it takes to be his caretaker have hindered her ability to tend to our concerns to some extent. But I don't complain, because I understand why.

I think Sarah and Penelope understand that my mother eases a burden that would otherwise fall on them. Tom is a wonderful person, and so are his children. They love him to death, and having Sarah nearby in Boston is a good thing for Tom. But my mom's kids, we're all spread out and far away, so she doesn't have that support close by.

But the hard truth is that my mother's gotten a raw deal, especially after a difficult marriage and divorce, and I'm very bummed about that. You can move on after a divorce; you don't move on from this.

When I come home to visit, I see high anxiety. My mom's temper is a bit shorter; she gets very frustrated, and sometimes she snaps at Tom. I think this is simply a reflection of the toll his illness has taken on her.

I don't feel like there's much I can do to affect the situation one way or the other. That's one of the toughest parts, not being in control. That's the part that makes me angry, but I know it won't help anyone for me to get consumed by it.

* *

For Vicki's youngest child, my stepdaughter Olivia, powerlessness is also a predominant theme. Peering around the corner of our lives, her major worry is that her mother will be alone, literally and figuratively.

OLIVIA BAKER: Tom was such a breath of fresh air, compared to the other men my mother had dated. He didn't try to be anyone but himself, didn't try too hard. He was warm and inviting. When I first met him, he was a very active person. We'd play tennis, and I went to hear the band he played in, but now he's not doing those things any more.

When they first told us he had Parkinson's, we were on our way to my grandparents' for Thanksgiving. They asked us to keep it quiet, because no one was really sure what was going on. I didn't really know how to react. I didn't know anything about Parkinson's, and I hadn't noticed any changes in Tom, so it seemed somewhat abstract to me. It wasn't until some time later that I noticed changes. He'd send me a birthday card and I couldn't read his handwriting any more; it became harder to understand his speech; and sometimes he said things that seemed out of context. It was when my mom told me about Lewy body disease and what it was that I began to think, "Uh-oh, this could really be serious," and I started to wonder what the future would bring.

My mother's life has changed dramatically, and she isn't living the life she thought she would when she married Tom. That's the hardest thing for me. But they were meant for each other. My mother is very unselfish and very good at taking care of people. I think she's dealing with it very well. She wouldn't give Tom up for anything.

I don't have any anger about the situation; this is just how it has to be. My mom is still able to give me the same amount of love and attention she always has, though sometimes I think she is a little quicker to anger when I'm being annoying.

Sometimes when I'm home, my mom may ask me to help Tom with something, like program phone numbers into his cell phone. He wants me to show him how to do it, not to do it for him, even though I could do it much quicker myself and he gets frustrated. But I know he doesn't want to be dependent, and he's very appreciative.

I always hoped my mom would find someone, even though she's very independent. I want her to have someone to be with for the rest of her life. I haven't thought a lot about the future, because I'm afraid to go there and because my mother has always been the kind of person who seems to be able to take care of anything and ensure that it will work out fine. She's always been very good at protecting her children from difficult situations by projecting a sense of reassurance. She's always fixed problems quietly and quickly. But this is a problem that can't be fixed. I'm afraid my mom will be alone, either because Tom can't be home any more or because he could die. I don't know a lot about the disease and how it could progress.

Mostly I feel powerless to affect the situation. I live far away, and I don't know what I could do other than to be supportive of them both.

* *

Though I am the one losing control over my body and my mind, I realize that a sense of powerlessness has infiltrated Vicki's children's lives too. It's sobering to realize how much emotional energy is expended on my illness, the sense of vulnerability and uncertainty it has introduced into their young lives.

For Vicki's children, my illness is something foreign and mysterious, for they came to it with little exposure to medical problems. Their parents have always been healthy, so they have never feared losing a loved one to illness. Now, without warning, they have been thrust into an existence in which a bewildering, degenerative neurological disease has disrupted their lives, and it's hard for them to know how to respond.

The Prince Charming who was going to take their divorced mother into a romantic, fairytale future has, instead, introduced them to a nightmare. This is patently unfair, but there is little I can do to change it. The best thing I can do for them is to try to keep things light. I try to reassure them by projecting an air of normality, to the extent that I can. By showing them that I can still laugh and be playful, and by making our time together about something other than my illness, I seek to reassure them. My job with Vicki's kids is to try to break down their anxiety as best I can.

* * *

For my own children, it is an entirely different matter. I yield as little as possible to my illness, and I remain physically and socially active because I owe it to them, and to Vicki, to be the best I can be under my increasingly constrained circumstances. But for Penelope and Sarah, who lost their mother in 1998, this illness has a deeper meaning and presents a more formidable set of emotional challenges. I am their father, grandfather to their children, and the man they have looked to since the day they were born for stability, support, and love. I'm the father they helped nurture through their mother's death, and who, in turn, nurtured them through the same tragedy. And now they are slowly but inexorably losing me. The relationships between and among the three of us were always very intense. My illness has intensified them even more.

The way Penelope and Sarah experience my illness is shaped by the crucible of Caroline's illness and death. Though Penelope was in law school at Georgetown and Sarah in college at Wesleyan University during Caroline's illness, both were very involved in her care. They became adept at changing i.v.'s, managing medications, and mastering the myriad details of caretaking a terminally ill cancer patient with a feeding tube and oxygen tank. Together with their future husbands, Patrick and Tom, we forged the concept of "Team Graboys," sharing the burdens, physical and emotional, of caring for Caroline over nearly two exhausting, grief-stricken years. The girls moved home for long stretches and took over with exceptional dedication, caretaking not just Caroline, but their bereft father as well.

When Caroline took ill, she gave me complete control over the management of her illness. I was the physician; I would know how to maneuver through the thicket of medical decision-making and bureaucracy; I would be able to weigh the options both as a husband and a doctor. She committed to doing anything and everything we asked of her and was relieved not to have to orchestrate the day-to-day decision-making related to her care. In shifts we tended to her, twenty-four hours a day, seven days a week, taking turns to ensure that someone was always by her side, or at least in the house. If she needed her privacy, which she often did, she would bang her cane on the floor or ring the bell we left by her bedside when she needed us.

The early signs of Parkinson's and Lewy body disease began to manifest themselves, shortly after Caroline died, as forgetfulness, occasional confusion, and fatigue, all easily dismissed as symptoms of acute and chronic grief. Penelope and Sarah were concerned, and rightly so, that her death would lead to depression in me, and they wanted to be there to keep me from falling too far.

Penelope, my older daughter, also lives in California, and the physical distance between us makes my illness especially painful for her. Her plate is more than full. A partner at a major San Francisco law firm, and a mother of three young children, my illness has introduced an ongoing grief that is part of her daily life.

PENELOPE GRABOYS BLAIR: After my mother died, Sarah and I saw our dad a lot. We were very close during that time and relied on each other heavily. We also worried about our father's depression. Certain traits, certain eccentricities of his, seemed to be a little more pronounced. It wasn't dramatic, but it was enough to make us somewhat concerned. We were comforted by the fact that he continued to see his therapist and that he was taking antidepressants.

My father had an active social life; later, when he began dating, he was considered a very eligible bachelor. We viewed his social activities as a good sign. After my dad became engaged to Vicki, they decided to live together and to buy a new house where they could make a new start together. The process of packing up and selling the house where we had grown up seemed to be very unsettling and disruptive to our dad. How to go about the process seemed to elude him. He was always an exceptionally capable person, and when he started to slow down it was a relative matter—he still operated at a level of effectiveness beyond that of many others. Having grown up with him, it was noticeable to us, though understandable as a result of his depression.

He puttered around the house a lot, and when I would come up for a visit from New York I would find that he had done something Sarah and I did not understand, like throw out packets of love letters between him and my mother that he'd saved for decades. We would mark boxes "do not discard," but did not have total confidence that they would still be there when we came back. His decision-making seemed to be somewhat random. All these decisions, like throwing out love letters or family Christmas ornaments, however, could be explained more out of my dad's acting in grief, or out of respect for Vicki, than anything else.

Over the next couple of years after Vicki and my dad were married, there were subtle changes in our conversations, both by telephone and in person, such as changing the subject in the middle of a statement. With hindsight, I now know it was a way for him to mask the fact that he was struggling for a word or had lost his train of thought. He had always been such a good listener and so engaged and always able to give me, or others, comfort or advice. But at the time I'm referring to, there were increasingly occasions when I would share a problem or a story and he would not respond in a meaningful way. Over time, it became progressively worse. At times, he seemed disengaged from the conversation, which was so unlike him. Until he was diagnosed, we suspected that he was depressed. Now I understand that it was a symptom of the Parkinson's.

Today we face a new reality. Our dad is retired. I live in San Francisco and have three young children. In many ways, my mother's illness and death have prepared us to deal with this. In some ways, I have come to understand that one does not really become an adult until one loses a parent, and Sarah and I are more weathered and scarred as a result of our mother's death. Sarah and I wonder whether we are better prepared to handle loss and mourning and trauma within the family because we've been through it before. We have certainly learned to cherish each moment together. Before my mother's illness, we felt like the perfect family. Ultimately, we didn't get perfection. Over time after my mother passed away, the three of us—Sarah, my dad, and I— thought that as long as we had each other, we would be able to build a new future together. So we carry a lot of emotional baggage into this scenario with our dad.

He knows we are battle-weary, and he is determined to avoid burdening us, but I worry that he might feel like he's getting the short end of the stick from us because we expended so much in the battle for my mother.

The biggest immediate adjustment for me is having to lower my expectations for the level of our communication. We always had such good communication lines, and our conversations, from the time I was young, were substantial and deep. Despite his challenges, he continues to be an incredible listener and supporter, but while he still clearly shows us how much he cares and supports us, letting go of the type of conversations we used to have has been a real loss for me. Over time, there will certainly be other, more significant, adjustments for me and our whole family.

There are many things I would be speaking about with my dad if he was healthy, but you do not want to worry someone and burden them with your problems when they are struggling with such profound problems of their own. I try to time my telephone calls to my dad so that I catch him at a good time during the day. He has a hard time on the telephone and knows it, but we are getting better.

Infantilization of the seriously ill is something Sarah and I are very much aware of—we heard my dad speak, over many years, about elderly patients losing control over their lives and the regression that often occurs. When my mother was ill, lines of responsibility in our family started to shift a bit as we took care of her and began managing the household too. This continued after my mother died. We are very sensitive about this with respect to my dad.

One of the most painful issues for me relates to my own children, who are very young now. We make sure we see my dad as much as we can, and I try to appreciate every drop of good time he has with his grandchildren, and I know he gives them the very best he can give. I desperately want them to know what a remarkable, talented, engaging, and special person my dad is. I think there is a lot that goes on in my dad's mind that he doesn't show, and his appreciation for his grandchildren is evident. I sometimes wish we had the 1992 version of him, in that his relationship with my children would be different, but my mother never knew her grandchildren at all and we can only share pictures and stories. To them, she is something of an angel. They can't see her, but we work very hard at making her presence felt in their lives. That is why I appreciate every single moment my children have with my dad, who is a very real and important figure in their lives.

It is a wonderful thing for my dad that he has Vicki in his life, in many ways. We deeply appreciate what Vicki does in caring and loving my dad. She is a tremendous person who is a wonderful, loving caregiver. It is an enormous relief to my sister and me. It also brings forth a lot of guilt, because if Vicki were not in my dad's life he would be living with Sarah or me, it would have happened years ago, and Sarah and I would be taking care of him. I feel guilty that I am not doing the same things for my dad that I did for my mother, but he seems to prefer it this way. At this stage, perhaps, it would be harder for him if Sarah and I were taking care of him. He has made clear how concerned he is about burdening us and that it is easier for him to accept help from Vicki and retain his role as father and not become dependent on us. But it is hard in some ways for us to have him so dependent on someone else, rather than on us. However, we are not going anywhere, and both Sarah and I count on continuing to make this a team effort with Vicki.

The future is the biggest question for all of us. We all want to be closer together, but the geographic situation is the $64,000 question. It is easy—and selfish—to say that my dad and Vicki should move out here, especially since Vicki has two children who live in San Francisco. But Vicki has her work and social support in Boston, as does my dad. They will have to make the decision that is best for them. This is my daily torture, being so far away from my dad.

* *

My son-in-law, Patrick, is much more to me now than my daughter's husband. He is a friend who has helped all of us through extraordinarily difficult times, first Caroline's death and now my illness.

PATRICK BLAIR: My relationship with Tom has not changed significantly as a result of his Parkinson's. When I first met Tom, Penelope and I were seniors at Cornell and it was graduation weekend. He was the typical protective father, skeptical about me, and I was intimidated by him. Caroline was very friendly, and so I tried to spend as much time with her as possible. At dinner one night, there were a lot of us around the table and Tom ended up sitting across from me. He had not said anything to me at this point. When it came time to order, I chose a steak and a beer, and the first thing he said to me was, "Do you know the average man gains twenty-five pounds after college graduation?" He was giving me a hard time, but I was not sure how much he was jesting with me or how much he was testing me. He knew what he was doing. He was reserving judgment, as a good father should.

In the years since, we have become very close. Tom was always ready to play, especially tennis. That was one of his biggest passions. It would be 110 degrees and humid outside, but he would persuade me to go out and play with him. As the boyfriend, I was an easy target. Tom is a guy's guy. We have a lot of laughs and continue to have a good time together. To me, the issue of moving to be closer to Tom has less to do with his Parkinson's than with the realities of aging. Penelope and I think about the same thing with my parents. It is part of being a family as parents age. We have a lot of friends dealing with the same types of issues. As Tom changes, the family will have to adapt, but it is a challenge that many families face. The Parkinson's, however, intensifies and accelerates the issue.

Penelope is an incredible woman, as is Sarah. In the years since their mother died, Penelope graduated from law school, became the youngest partner at a San Francisco law firm, married, and had three children; and she's a star in all her roles—as lawyer, wife, mother, and daughter to Tom. This is a woman with a great capacity to deal with tremendous demands. Her tank is never empty.

The hardest part of dealing with Tom's illness is being so far away. If we lived nearer, it would ease some of the emotional burden for Penelope. Tom would never want us to move just for him. We would love to have him move here, but not just because of his illness. It would be good to be closer for many reasons. As of now, I don't have fear or anxiety about his condition worsening, though I know it will intensify all of these issues for us.

In a perfect world, I wish my children could see Tom as he was when I first met him, and that they could meet Caroline. I try to focus on being happy with the time Tom gets to spend with his grandchildren. He was in the delivery room within fifteen minutes of the births of our children. I can't imagine most grandfathers doing that. This was a real gift for me and for my children.

Rigby, our eldest, knows so much about Tom from stories Tom tells him. Tom has told him about flying gliders in his Air Force days. Rigby knows his grandfather is an esteemed doctor. He knows Tom did some work in Africa. Many kids have aging grandparents who can't necessarily do everything they used to do, or never knew their grandparents at all. But Tom has been able to share a lot with Rigby. I try to look at the positive side. We can still do a lot

together. When they were here over the holidays, we all
went to the Emerald Bowl [a college football game] and
had a great time.

There is no disputing how incredibly difficult the situation is for him and for so many people who love him. I hate
to see how frustrated Tom gets, and seeing the disease
progress is very hard and taxing. We are grateful for every
day, and I still see a lot of the same guy I always knew in him.

Tom can still be so funny. When he was here, Jen's husband [Vicki's son-in-law], Micah, took Tom to an indoor firing range where Tom shot a .357 Magnum at targets. No
one appreciated the irony and humor in a Parkinson's
patient armed with a .357 Magnum trying to hit a target
more than Tom did. I gather they typically get quite a different crowd there; and when he came back, he said, "I think
it's safe to say that I was the only sixty-two-year-old Jewish
cardiologist with Parkinson's there."

Penelope and Sarah spend an enormous amount of time
and energy making sure their dad continues to be doing
what he needs to do to take care of himself. They have a
remarkably open and communicative family. It is a very adult
relationship among them. There is nothing they won't say to
one another, and that really helps them through this.
Regardless of how difficult this is for Tom and our family,
worse things could happen. He is here, and we cherish and
hold on to that.

* *

My younger daughter, Sarah, recently began her career as an equine veterinarian and gave birth to her first child. Because she lives near Boston, we are fortunate to be able to see each other frequently. Like her sister, she is fiercely devoted and protective of me. We have always been exceptionally close, and she mourns the loss of the dad she grew up with.

SARAH GRABOYS VALEO: Fundamentally, I always come back to the feeling that my father's illness is a loss for everyone. The medical profession and his patients have lost an exceptionally devoted and compassionate doctor—and, of course, it's such a loss for his family and for him. When I have a "poor me" moment about my own feelings of loss, I think about the fact that it must be infinitely more difficult for my dad to have to acknowledge what is happening—the physical and mental changes, his desperately wanting to maintain his independence, the fear about the future. What a loss it is for him; it must be so hard.

I feel as though I have lost my father in some ways. There are parallels with the loss of my mother, but it's different. My mother kept her mental faculties through most her illness, then went through a rapid senility. It was like seeing her old age compressed into a short time. With Dad, the changes are more subtle and are progressing more slowly. But in both cases, I have felt my own role change from that of child to nurturer and caretaker.

My dad and I have always had a special connection. I think we have similar temperaments, and we have a common interest in medicine, and that may explain why we have been so close. He was always my "go-to" guy. Whatever the problem, whatever the issue I needed help with, we could always talk freely, candidly, and in depth. The great listening skills he brought to medicine, he brought home as well. I could really lean on him and depend on him. It's been an easy relationship and an uncomplicated one.

The loss I feel over dad's illness is most acute when big decisions come up. I can't go to him any more, the way I used to. Penelope and I search for something from him, something parental, but it's hard for him to be the parent we depended on for so long. He can't engage us the way he used to, especially on the phone. On the phone it's really impossible. So there's this sense of yearning for that parent-child connection that eludes us. When I do seek him out for advice, the conversations tend to be half-conversations. Some days he says things that are so poignant, but on other days the connection just isn't there. On any given day when I go to see him, I always hope I will be able to glimpse the father I grew up with. It's a new "normal," and it is hard to adjust to.

As soon as my mother got sick and then died, the dynamic in our family changed dramatically. Our relationship with Dad went from parent-child to an adult-to-adult relationship. It happened earlier for us than most people. We found ourselves doing things children don't normally do for their parents at such a young age, especially the caretaking. I lived at home throughout all of my mother's illness. I went to every chemotherapy appointment and many others. And

after she died, I stayed home and lived with my dad.
Penelope and I saw up-close the raw emotion of death and
of loss in Dad. The whole experience drew us so much
tighter, and we were already close; and we came to know
Dad more intimately than most kids will ever know their
parents. So as my dad's illness plays out, there is an intensity
about the experience for all of us that is heightened by what
we went through with my mom. But, having been through
my mother's illness, I think I take my father's more in stride.
I know we will get through it, that we are a strong family,
and that we can handle whatever comes down the road.

I try not to flip the parent-child relationship with my
dad. I try to treat him the same way I always have, but it's not
always possible. I'm always on his case to make sure he's
doing everything he's supposed to be doing—whether he's
had enough water and whether he's taking his medications.
I ask him whether he's fallen, a common occurrence these
days that has resulted in quite a few bumps and bruises. I zip
his coat for him, and I give him the once-over when comes
out of the bathroom to make sure he's zipped up and put
together. We try to laugh about it, and I try not to make him
self-conscious about it. We realize there's something absurd
about my needing to give him a visual inspection, but I
know that each of these small things chips away at his sense
of independence and self-esteem.

If Dad didn't have Vicki in his life, Penelope and I would
be living with him, or very nearby. They never imagined
that something like this could happen to them, especially

not so quickly and at such a relatively young age. It's terribly unfair; but in any marriage you never know what can happen, and you sign on for better or worse. I am sure that if their situations were reversed, Dad would be doing as much for Vicki as she is for him. And despite his limitations, I think Dad does a lot, in different ways, for Vicki. I think each of them makes the other a better person. Vicki is just great with my dad; I can't imagine a better caretaker. But I worry that we are not there enough for her, both emotionally and to help out. I am in the process of moving and starting a new job, and once we are settled I hope I can do more to spell her.

My life is more difficult than I thought it would be. I never imagined that I'd have lost my mother by this point in my life and dealing with my father being ill too. My husband and I are both very committed to our families, and his family is nearby in Newburyport. So we sometimes feel like it's a struggle to carve out space for ourselves and to put our own small family first.

Our time now is precious. His dementia has progressed, but there is still a lot we can do together. He still enjoys the movies, sporting events, his music, and seeing family. There's still a lot of spark, though less than there once was. There's still much we can enjoy together; and despite how angry and frustrated he is by his illness, he still laughs, often at his own expense. Even before he became ill, whenever I thought my dad was slipping into one of his narcissistic moments I would put a finger up in the air and draw a circle around his head.

The idea was the whole world revolves around dad. It was a good-natured way of pulling him out of his self-indulgent moments, and it still works.

I worry about the future all the time. What's going to happen? It's the great unknown. My husband, Tom, and I are tied to the area as long as Dad is here, that's for certain. There's talk of everyone moving to San Francisco, and that could happen. But wherever we are, Dad will never be anyplace but home.

★ ★

Sarah's husband, Tom Valeo, is another gem whose steadiness and emotional generosity helps us all keep our heads above water. He, too, is more than a son-in-law. He's been a genuine friend.

TOM VALEO: At the end of the day, all I can do is provide companionship and support to Tom. He doesn't want our relationship to change because he has Parkinson's. My role is to continue our friendship as it was, the best I can.

Some things have changed. We used to play basketball and tennis. He loved tennis. It was a family affair, and he would play as much as he possibly could. If you came over and were watching TV or reading the paper, Tom would walk in dressed for tennis, racquet and ball in hand, and start bouncing the ball in front of you until you succumbed. It was like he was saying "come play with me." That's missing now. He also loved to ski, but we can't do that either. But he's replaced some of that with spinning and working out. He's done an amazing job to try and stay fit.

Sarah's feelings bottom out sometimes about it. There's something missing for her. She wants to be there to help, but Tom is on an island a bit. Penelope and Sarah both really like to talk things out to the *n*th degree, and they have a lot of questions for Tom about many things—about his meds, about what shoes he was wearing when he fell, whether he's doing this or that or the other thing. It can be exhausting; and in phone calls with Tom they seek a lot, but he can't reciprocate. Tom is still a healer. He has great bedside manner and is very keyed-in to the needs of others, but he can't always respond to those needs as he used to.

The Graboys house was always filled with deep, detailed debates about many things, but especially ethical debates about law and medicine. Tom thrived on it. He loved to debate serious issues, but that's missing now. But he taught his children to ask questions. That was the legacy of all those discussions.

When I see him, I think he likes to "pretend" the disease isn't there. He tries to keep the normal banter going. He's a guy's guy, and he likes to maintain that in our relationship. He just wants to be involved in your life. It's got to be hard to maintain your interest in others when you are living with a disease like this, but he really does. I've always asked Tom for advice. When my sister died, I confided in him. I've asked his advice about my career and about life in general. He doesn't make demands, and he never puts any pressure on us in any way.

Vicki does so much for Tom and he does the same for her. Vicki really makes his life as easy as it can be for him, but to make it easy is hard work for her. He uses his sense of humor to deflect the stress, and that's one of the biggest things he does for her and for all of us. He helps all of us keep his disease in perspective. It's one of the things we all love about him; he knows how to defuse tense situations. Vicki is always concerned about how much sugar he's eating, so he buys Tootsie Rolls and leaves wrappers around the house for Vicki to find. He still loves to play.

★ ★

The most painful thing about these statements, what I was least prepared for, is the degree to which my dementia has progressed. The picture painted of my ability to connect and communicate is worse than I imagined. It's a bitter pill to swallow.

I want to be their "go-to" guy, as I once was. Though I can still muster the residual intellectual firepower to offer sound medical guidance, my ability to engage, to give fatherly advice as I once did, is diminished. I would welcome the chance to commiserate with my daughters over their problems, whatever they are. But while I can give them the same measure of love I always gave them, I cannot communicate with them as I once did.

Because dementia makes it hard for me to read myself, to know how others perceive my interactions with them, and to appreciate the extent of my own deficits, these candid but heartfelt statements are a harsh reality check. How do we accept this? How do we accept that only remnants remain of the father they once knew?

Penelope and Sarah talk every day to share every observation, incident, and interaction we have had, constantly and exhaustively monitoring me so they can devise strategies they hope will make things better for me, even at the margins. Am I taking my medications as prescribed? Am I staying hydrated? Have I fallen? How is my driving? Have I noticed any changes in myself? Constantly on guard against my lapsing into self-pity, they use humor and candor to keep me in the game. They still give me a hard time and make me the brunt of their jokes. This intense involvement is therapeutic for them and for me. Being proactive helps fend off their feelings of helplessness, and I, in turn, am reassured by their visceral wherewithal to persevere in these difficult circumstances.

Their need to know everything that goes on in my life is also an effort to bring order to chaos. Both are very powerful and determined women, like their mother, and tenacious. They are fiercely protective and intensely devoted. But their vigilance also reflects their worry about losing their only remaining parent, that mooring that helps deflect us from focusing too intently on our own mortality. You can gird yourself against the loss of one parent, but it's much harder to prepare yourself for the loss of the second. I, too, worry that my children, even though they are grown women, will be "orphaned." In some respects, Caroline's death scene is being replayed in slow motion as my dementia progresses, and it is possible that they may be figuratively orphaned if I am here physically but not mentally.

Penelope and Sarah's vigilance also reflects their awareness of how large a role denial has played in my life, especially in the early years of my illness. They don't quite trust me to be completely forthcoming with information they feel they need to help me manage my illness, so they question me rigorously and in detail. Sometimes I find it exhausting, but I understand why they do it and I am grateful for it. But they walk a fine line between trying not to treat me like a child and wanting to be, as I want them to be, an integral part of my care and management of my disease. Their daily presence in my life, their advocacy and cheerleading, and their sheer competence is salutary and a source of great comfort.

While Penelope and Sarah are better prepared and battle-hardened by previous experience, they have never, since the day Caroline was diagnosed, enjoyed a reprieve from serious illness or known a life in which they didn't fear for their parents. I am sorry that the early years of starting their own families and careers have been burdened by illness and worry and caretaking, but that is our reality and there is no escaping it. But they know, because they have been down this road before, that they will survive, that they are strong, and that "Team Graboys," now expanded to include Vicki and her children, is still intact to face my illness. That was the concept behind "Team Graboys" from the beginning—that we would shore one another up, do everything we could to keep one another healthy, and find strength in our numbers.

But how do I tell them *everything* without adding to their burden? Do I share my despair? I naturally want to protect my children, and yet I want them to face reality and to help them feel as much control as they can in a situation that is inherently uncontrollable. I do confide in them when I am not feeling well, but some aspects of illness, no matter how strong the support structure around you, are borne alone—not sharing every dark moment, every morbid thought, and every fear is how the ill can help ease the burden of the well.

My children and grandchildren are a major part of what motivates me to do all that I do to push back against my illness—the exercise, the travel, and the high level of social activity. I owe it to all of them, Vicki, and our extended family to do everything I can to be as healthy as I can be for as long as I can. This is another way I can ease their burden. When they see me staying active, it is reassuring and therapeutic for them, too. Though Penelope and Sarah worry that I may push myself too hard and that something catastrophic will happen, on balance, maintaining a high level of activity shows them that I am still in the game. As people move into old age or endure an advancing illness and suffer the erosion of their activities of daily living, it is common to become involuted and withdrawn. I guard against that, using my family, and especially my daughters, as my motivation to not surrender to illness. The struggle to remain engaged and active requires an enormous expenditure of energy, physical and emotional, and simply becomes overwhelming at times, but that is now my full-time job.

* * *

One of the most poignant issues for me, as well as for Penelope and Sarah, is my relationship with my grandchildren. Penelope and Patrick have three children, Rigby, four, Nick, two, and Carson, born in September of 2007; and Sarah and Tom's child, Walker, was born in October 2007. I, too, appreciate every drop of time I can get with them. I just want them to know me as best as they can, given my limitations.

On a visit to San Francisco over a year ago, I picked Rigby up at daycare and took him out for lunch. He is just beginning to have a sense that Pops can't do everything the other adults in his life do, yet he is remarkably patient. I wonder: Does he know, intuitively, that I need his patience? When it was time to go, I tried to help him into his jacket, and he ended up with both arms in one sleeve, and no amount of fumbling on my part could sort it out. But he didn't fuss; he waited until someone passing by lent a hand. And he didn't complain when I became confused on the public bus system and landed us twenty blocks from our destination and I carried him, both of us exhausted, for ten blocks before finding the bus that would take us home. (In the scramble that is often my brain, the logistics of mass transit have become too complex.) I, too, wish he had the 1992 version of me, because I cannot be the grandfather we all would have envisioned—the one that could take his grandchildren skiing, or read books to them, have animated conversations over the phone, or go places together by car.

* * *

Will I, in a year, two years, or five, be able to interact and function—as a father, husband, and grandfather? What happens if I am not able to take care of myself and become totally dependent? What will that do to all these family relationships? Will they stay intact? Will they break apart under the pressure? Will they grow even stronger? This is the pervasive fear, and these are the unanswerable, overwhelming questions.

I cannot exorcise the anxiety and fear that this dementia will progress to the point where Vicki can't handle me any more. My daughters have vowed—and they are capable and strong enough to do so—to never have me be anywhere but home; if not with Vicki, then with them. But do I want that for *them*? Is this what awaits us? We simply don't know. I would happily accept my current state of dementia, and I would accept Parkinson's, if I knew that the dementia would remain static. That's a bargain I would take. But there's no one with whom I can make that deal.

I worry, too, about the emotional toll my illness takes on my daughters day to day, and how it saps the energy they need to devote to their husbands and children. I am concerned that everyone around me—Vicki, my kids, and hers—will get worn down emotionally over time; that as the disease progresses, the toll will be greater and greater. How deep is the emotional reservoir? One of the most common statements made by all patients is "I don't want to be a burden." But unless you are blessed with a quick exit, the seriously ill patient *will* impose burdens on his family.

* * *

If I was unprepared for the reality check on my ability to interact with my children, I was also quite unprepared for the Pandora's box that was opened when I asked the kids to share their feelings about my illness for this book. Though little goes unsaid in our family, it isn't said for public consumption; and my daughters, in particular, are struggling with my desire to share our very personal story. They know it is important to me for many reasons—to make something of value out of my illness, to

continue to "doctor" to others in some way, to take on an intellectual challenge when my mind is beginning to desert me—yet
the process has been painful for them. Is it fair or right for me
to tell a story that they would rather not make public? Am I
thrusting this book on my family unfairly? Is it arrogant? Self-
indulgent? Am I adding to the burden my illness has already
imposed by dragging them through this process? And, if so, do
my needs trump theirs?

* * *

My disease has put everyone in my immediate and extended families into a state of vigilance, hoping for the best but preparing for
the worst. We are living with this great unknown; closure is elusive, because outcomes are not predictable. How could you not
feel guilt about the anguish your illness causes others? But you
have to ask yourself: If I expend a lot of energy on this, will it
make things better? So I guard against self-pity and despair as best
I can (though I am not always successful), but that is all I can do.

One recent evening, as Vicki was standing at the kitchen sink
loading the dishwasher, she started to sob. I asked her what was
wrong, and she said she was just so incredibly, deeply sad. It was
one of those moments when the full enormity and tragedy of
our life washed over Vicki like a wave. At the core, for each
member of our family, there is an inconsolable sadness lodged
like a sword cemented in stone. From the center of our family
on out, sadness owns the day.

SIX

Friends

SOME FRIENDSHIPS LAST a lifetime, some less. Some have the intensity of a marriage, while others may lack intimacy but provide camaraderie. Some are built around work, some around a shared experience such as childhood, college, or child-rearing, and others around games—tennis friends, running friends, ski friends. Some friends you can spend a week traveling with, some would drive you crazy after a day. Some friendships survive separations of time and space, while others hang on, barely, like a reluctant leaf in late fall, only to wither and die. Some friendships survive serious illness, others do not, but all are changed by it.

Caroline's cancer and death, and now my Parkinson's and dementia, have reordered my social universe. They have brought some old friends to deeper levels of caring and intimacy, and resurrected at least one friendship that had been attenuated by the passing of the years. Illness has even borne some new friendships in which the common struggle with life-changing disease is the bond. Other friendships, some which centered on activities I can no longer join, such as tennis and medical practice, and others with people I once held dear, have petered out.

Dementia, by its very nature, challenges friendships in unique ways because communication, the lifeblood of any relationship, is compromised, and because the disease chips away at what makes you who you are. Not only have all my friendships been reshaped by my illness; in many ways, each has become centered around it. People adjust to the new you, but the relationship can never be the same, and as the dementia progresses each relationship gradually changes with it. As I lose incremental parts of myself, those around me lose parts of me as well.

I cannot be the same kind of friend I once was, because I cannot engage intellectually as I once did or participate in many of the activities I once enjoyed. My fatigue and other symptoms limit what I can do socially. Friends have to be more mindful and aware in their interactions with me, more tuned in so they can make sense of my often halting, sometimes jumbled conversation, and infinitely more patient. But try as they might, especially in group social situations, life must eventually return to normal speed, even if it means I sometimes get left behind. That's why I often lean on discussion of other people's medical issues to sustain conversation—it is ground on which I am steady and still knowledgeable, and it allows me to compensate for my inability to keep up in other areas. And people like to talk about themselves and their ailments. Among friends, I derive a great deal of gratification from helping people with their medical problems: arranging a referral, giving general advice, talking about interesting cases I have had.

But I also have many casual encounters with acquaintances where medical talk evokes an entirely different reaction. I often run into acquaintances who ask, "So, Tom, how are you doing?" After a few words from me ("I'm fine"), in an effort to reassure me, well-meaning people will begin telling me their medical woes, the medications they are taking, or that they, too, have become forgetful or absent-minded. They believe there is solace for me in their stories, but there isn't. "Believe me," I want to say, "your occasional forgetfulness doesn't make me feel better about my advancing dementia, and anyway they don't compare." I don't mind answering their medical questions; indeed, that makes me feel useful. But I don't want to be a repository for people's complaints and I don't want them to patronize me or minimize my symptoms by making facile comparisons to their own. So, over time, I have slowly moved away from those who think they are lightening my burden by sharing their own, preferring to engage with people who avoid light banter in favor of more meaningful dialogue.

* * *

To understand my social world now, you have to know something about it before—before cancer took Caroline, and before Parkinson's and dementia started to take me.

During our marriage, our social life was largely built around Caroline's remarkable broad array of friendships, many dating back to college and graduate school, some forged during her twin careers as a museum director and a mother, and others that grew out of her time as a political activist and one-time candidate for the Massachusetts legislature.

In Boston, where medicine is a major industry, the socializing among doctors who work in the city's leading institutions tends to reflect the city's intense and complicated medical politics, where maneuvering for professional advantage is both an art form and a contact sport. Though I have, over the years, made some very dear friends in the medical community, I had little interest in the medical social scene. Besides, the work culture already demanded superhuman commitment. I regularly worked eighty hours a week or more, especially in the early stages of my career. With precious little time for my wife and children, nurturing friendships inside or outside the medical community was not a priority. I was happy to cede control over our social calendar to Caroline.

Outgoing, attractive, fiercely intelligent, and emotionally generous, she was a magnet for people and our social circle was extensive. But there were six women in particular who coalesced into a very tight-knit core group of friends around Caroline. They went away together several times a year, and the men, with our kids, would get together in their absence for what was supposed to be a bonding experience. Perhaps it was for the others, but it wasn't for me. By nature somewhat reserved, I had difficulty integrating with the men and, because I was working so hard and had so little time alone with my children, I preferred to be with Penelope and Sarah, just the three of us. Though we saw some of the women and their husbands as couples from time to time, I had no strong independent relationships with the individuals in Caroline's "women's group."

Caroline was the center of gravity in this tight circle, the "go-to" girl if you had an emergency, a crisis, a question, or a problem. She was the first among equals. The women bonded around illnesses (Caroline was not the first among them to have a serious health problem) and other life crises—marital problems, career crises, and the like.

Selfless to a fault, her generosity was repaid during her illness with extraordinary love and devotion from her women's group. They provided near round-the-clock companionship when Caroline wanted it, understood when she needed to be alone;

and at 2 A.M. on the night she died, as Caroline had requested, they came, bathed her body, and dressed her in a plain white shroud, a scene of heartbreaking tenderness.

There were countless invitations to dinner in the months after she died and general well-intentioned offers to help, the kind of offers that often break under their own weight because there is a mutual understanding that nothing but time can really help lift the unbearable grief. In those first few weeks and months, I rebuffed so many overtures—from Caroline's friends and others—that many people simply gave up. I hunkered down—with my daughters as my safe haven—and often wandered our big house alone when I wasn't at work. I felt that going out and socializing would be pointless. What was there to talk about, if not Caroline? With the sun gone, the planets wobbled out of orbit. Despite everyone's best intentions, theirs and mine, my relationship with this group of women (and their husbands), which had been so central to Caroline's life for more than two decades, began to dissipate almost immediately after her death. Today, because of my dementia, I struggle to recall all their names; if I see any of them, it is purely a chance encounter.

Parkinson's and dementia have also redrawn my own social circle. The connections to colleagues with whom I worked for decades have dissipated for the simple reason that we no longer work side by side for sixty hours a week. Though built almost entirely around our professional lives together, I miss those friendships and the collegiality of the office. Other people, mostly couples, who Caroline and I knew over the years have quietly slipped out of my orbit through no one's fault; time and circumstance—theirs and mine—have loosened the ties that once bound us.

Though many friendships have not survived illness, others have—and have been deepened and enriched by it. I mean no disrespect to the many good friends who have remained close in my life through this ordeal, but I have chosen to write about only two who represent what is best in all of them.

* * *

Roger Levy was a friend from Cornell who settled with his wife, Sue, in Connecticut. Roger, a businessman and successful writer, was a senior in my freshman year and was like a second older brother to me. He took great pride in my becoming a doctor and in following my career. We became so close over the years that in 1988, while I was out of the country, Roger stood in for me as Penelope's "father" on a special father's weekend while she was attending Cornell.

In the early 1980s, when Sue was diagnosed with ovarian cancer, I helped answer the many questions they had about managing her illness, and Caroline spent days at a stretch tending to her, driving to Connecticut and staying at their house, a kindness Roger has never forgotten.

Roger remarried relatively soon after Sue died, and though we remained in touch, we didn't have as close a relationship with Roger and his new wife as we had had before. The four of us had a history dating back to college that couldn't be replicated. Gradually we saw less and less of Roger, though we never lost touch entirely. But when Caroline became ill, Roger started to call regularly to lend his moral and emotional support, and to reenter our lives in a sustained way.

During one of Caroline's hospitalizations, he flew up to Boston for the day to see me. Some friendships are easily re-kindled because the affection never wanes, the bond is too much a part of your DNA; and that is what happened with Roger. We sat together in the cafeteria at Brigham and Women's Hospital and had a long talk. Having experienced the same tragic events that now had us in their grip, Roger had much wisdom and empathy to share. "You are going to go through some terrible times," he said to me, both of us aware that Caroline was near-ing the end. He would be there—in any way, at any time—to help me through them, he said. Then, partly to explain himself, I think, but mostly to reassure me that my life would go on, he said, "Tom, Sue and I had a wonderful relationship, as do you and Caroline. But there is nothing wrong with remarrying if you find the right woman."

There are some things that only a very close friend can say, especially in times of grief and loss, and this was one of them. I wasn't taken aback, because Roger said it with such honesty and with great love and caring. That he could speak the unspeakable to me was, in some peculiar way, hopeful.

In fact, Caroline and I had discussed this very topic several times before. She was quite clear that she wanted me to remarry some day, but she had certain criteria: The woman should be about our age (no fall-spring romances) and should get along well with Penelope and Sarah. Remarriage can be a testament to the first marriage; for, if you had a strong first marriage, you are more likely to want to marry again.

Since Caroline's death, and even more so since my diagnosis, Roger, who now lives in New York City, calls me regularly to check in, to talk, and to offer comfort. He exudes a calm steadiness that I find reassuring and has a wonderful sense of humor that I enjoy. This may not sound like a lot, but the regularity of his calls, the tone of his voice, and the sincerity of his concern have brought me closer to Roger than ever. There is nothing perfunctory or obligatory about his calls or his conversation. His warmth and caring come across clearly, even over the phone, and I have the sense that he doesn't just care *about* me, but that he feels *for* me.

* * *

Everyone on a journey through serious illness should have a Jeffrey and Susan Sussman. Also friends since college, we were an inseparable quartet until Caroline died, sharing family vacations, holidays, and much else over the years.

Jeffrey and Susan were among the very first to notice that something was amiss with me. Shortly after Vicki and I were married, we spent a weekend with them in New York. They phoned Vicki almost immediately afterward to tell her something was wrong, and though neither has a background in medicine, they suspected it was neurological. Vicki was dumbfounded and alarmed. She had heard similar concerns from my friends Gilbert Mudge and John Rutherford, and now she was hearing it from Jeffrey and Susan. She had been puzzled by my inability to set a table properly, but she just chalked it up to the fact that as a busy doctor I had never had to assume such mundane chores. And since I was new in her life, what others saw as suspicious symptoms, she saw as idiosyncrasies and simple disorganization, though as time went by she started asking me about my lapses. But knowing me as well as they do, Jeffrey and Susan picked up quickly on my early symptoms.

Jeffrey is one of the most proactive people I know, a hard-charging real estate developer with a Midas touch and a gruff, no-nonsense exterior. Susan is his polar opposite: soft-spoken, gentle in word and kind, and easy-going. They are wonderful together. Until a few years ago, Jeffrey rarely, if ever, let his vulnerability show, and he was not given to "touchy-feely" conversations. I was always a bit envious of him: He always seemed so in-charge, so exceptionally competent and confident, and despite all I achieved over the years, I never entirely shed my insecurity.

Caroline's illness and death changed all of us, but most noticeably Jeffrey. The moment he learned of her diagnosis back in 1996, he came to Boston carrying a huge stuffed animal and vowing to do whatever he could for us. He was like an eager soldier ready to join in our battle. Our grief over Caroline—his, Susan's, and mine—was openly shared.

Then, just two days after Caroline's funeral, another shock: Jeffrey was diagnosed with lymphoma. I was already back at work trying to submerge my grief when Susan called me with the biopsy results. I canceled the rest of my appointments that day and caught the next flight to New York.

During Jeffrey's illness, he would often call to discuss the medical issues involved, and we would find ourselves baring our souls about our fears, our hopes, and our respective trials and tribulations with illness, treatments, and death; but it really was all about hearing the sound of each other's voice and knowing that we were in these struggles together. Jeffrey's search for the best doctor to treat his lymphoma was never-ending; it was in his makeup to always push for more information, the latest treatment, the doctor with the best statistical outcomes. Methodical and relentless, he brought these qualities to bear in pursuit of his own care. He had a large network of friends and acquaintances, including me, whose knowledge he tapped in his search, and he exhausted them all. (Today he is doing fine, and his prognosis is excellent.)

When I became ill, Jeffrey turned those same prodigious energies with the same intensity to me; Susan, likewise, with her gentle, concerned manner. Jeffrey had a seemingly endless series of names of physicians for me to consider to treat my Parkinson's. He called everyone he knew, seeking out suggestions, contacts, and information. He read up on the latest treatments, the newest drugs, and the clinical trials. He was my hard-charging advocate. It was as if he had the disease himself. Even though I was comfortable with Dr. Growdon, the knowledge that Jeffrey was spending time behind the scenes working my case and always thinking, thinking, thinking of how he could make things better was very gratifying. I certainly felt loved.

Having been through the mill of serious illness themselves, Jeffrey and Susan have been able to draw on their own experience to convey a sense of concern and support that is enormously reassuring. Serious illness can be a very lonely experience. Ultimately, no matter how expansive our support system, we are sometimes very much alone with our illness; but as long as Jeffrey and Susan are in my life, I will never be truly alone.

What differentiates Jeffrey and, in particular, Susan from those who are diligent merely about calling and saying the right things, is subtle. It's their ability to listen carefully and to move gently beyond the routine, predictable questions and answers. It's their attentiveness, which allows them, even by phone, to reach a deeper level of communion and convey an unmistakable empathy. When they ask what's going on or how I feel, they don't want superficial answers and won't accept them. Our discussions are often lengthy, and I am able to unburden myself with them in ways that I cannot with others. The whole range of my fears, anger, and concerns is part of our ongoing conversation and an important outlet, though I try to limit how much of my anxiety I convey, a skill I learned as a doctor. You may be alarmed about a patient's condition, but you don't want to communicate that alarm, for it can almost never have a positive effect. (There may be some circumstances where you need to alarm a patient who is failing, at great risk to themselves, to adhere to your recommendations. But otherwise, there is little to be gained by piling the doctor's anxieties onto the patient.) So, while Jeffrey and Susan offer an invaluable outlet, I try not to abuse the privilege.

* * *

Today, as in my first marriage, my social life revolves around my wife and her large circle of friends, none of whom knew the old Tom. As the only doctor in this group, I have found a comfortable niche as the focal point for all questions medical, that familiar territory where I can hide my impairment to some degree.

Among this group of good people, I have developed a special bond with one in particular, whom I'll call John. John is an impressive man, both physically and intellectually. He is witty, warm, charitable, and sensitive to those around him. He also suffers from life-threatening multiple myeloma, and our bond has been forged by our common battle with serious illness. When we see John and his wife, we talk about all the things you would expect of people our age: our children and grandchildren, politics, and current events. But then John and I almost always speak to each other of the common concerns we have about our illnesses: how our wives and children are coping, how we are coping, and the ups and downs of our treatments. Each of us has hit bottom emotionally over the past couple of years, and we find in one another a natural companion to share our anger, our grief, and our despair. I wish, of course, that John and I had become friends in good health, but our growing friendship is an example of how intimacy can develop through mutual illness. (As this book was going into production in September 2007, John passed away and I lost an important pillar of support.)

* * *

Ultimately, in illness, friendships, acquaintances, and family are our best defense against loneliness and isolation. As a physician, I was always more concerned about patients with little or no social support network than those who, despite a serious heart problem, were surrounded by attentive, empathetic family and friends. Those with companionship, a social network, and a sense of community simply have better medical outcomes, a testament to the power of positive human relationships on our physical and mental health. Loneliness and isolation can literally be heartbreakers.

But the presence of friends and family does more than assuage and comfort; it also, in many cases, helps the patient conduct him- or herself in illness with dignity and composure, because that is how the patient helps those around him or her cope with the illness. I try to conduct my life in ways that will help ease the burden of my illness on my family and my friends. They *expect* me to comport myself in ways that are consistent with who I was before my illness—Vicki calls it the essential gentleness of my nature—and so I do. It is what keeps me recognizable to others as the Tom they knew, and it helps me to keep from coming apart at the seams. So I try to keep my whining to a minimum, saving the existential rage for the therapist's office so it doesn't pollute my relationships with those closest to me.

Though I spend much time alone these days, I am not lonely. Already somewhat reclusive when my illness began, that tendency has been exacerbated. When I was working, I was constantly at the mercy of countless people who needed my time and attention. Now, though I detest the conditions that have forced me to retire into a more solitary existence, I cherish my time alone. In the cocoon of our home, there is no one to judge me, no one is watching me fumble with my coffee lid, and no one is asking me to bear the burden of their problems. At home, after Vicki, I am my own best friend.

SEVEN

A Body in Motion

THEY'VE CALLED MY NUMBER in the huddle. As we break, the center leans down over the ball and the linemen assume their three-point stance. I am a T-formation halfback, so I am lined up behind the quarterback. The quarterback, looking left, then right, barks out the signals. The ball is snapped, and the quarterback immediately begins his turn to the left as linemen collide in front of him. At exactly the same moment, I spring into motion, hands at the ready for what has to be a precise handoff. Any hesitation and I'll either fumble the ball or, worse, be set upon by half a dozen men much larger than me. I am small, even for a halfback, but quick and surefooted. I take the handoff smoothly as I accelerate into the rush of oncoming bodies. With the ball tucked firmly against my body with one arm, I begin pushing with the other against powerful bodies trying to knock me off my feet. One more quick step and I'll be home free; there is daylight ahead, and if I can dodge this last tackler it will be an open-field sprint to the end zone.

And that's the moment when I wake up and realize that the body I have been pushing against isn't a 200-pound lineman, but Vicki. It's another night of Lewy body–fueled dreams, those vivid episodes of REM sleep that summon my body into unconscious action. This time, fortunately, I've just been pushing, not punching or flailing like I often do.

The dream isn't altogether a bad one: For a brief moment, I have experienced the rush of feeling completely able-bodied.

My motions were fluid, my reflexes quick, and my muscles strong. But there is some disappointment, too: I woke up before I was able to break free and sprint to the end zone. The whole dream is an obvious metaphor for Parkinson's. I'm trying, I'm pushing myself forward in every way I know how, but ultimately there is no way to break free. When I wake, the fleeting exhilaration of the dream quickly gives way to reality.

* * *

Parkinson's has irrevocably altered my physical world and my place in it. In the most literal sense, the space in which I roam, delimited by the physical boundaries within which I live my life, has grown very small. It's not just that I can no longer drive, save to those two or three places where the route is etched into memory; it's also because I have lost the ability to navigate in unfamiliar places, and some places that were once familiar seem like foreign terrain. I am often lost in space, unsure of where I am and how to get to where I need to go (witness my adventure with my grandson Rigby in San Francisco), if indeed I can remember where I am going in the first place. It all leads to a deflating loss of self-confidence, a recognized syndrome associated with Parkinson's and old age.

Related, but distinct from this loss of confidence, is the loss of self-esteem that comes with being unable to move about at will, unable to master countless simple physical tasks of daily living, and the physical changes to my face and body that announce to the world that something is wrong with me.

And, finally, the way I experience the physical world is altered by the simple fact that I often feel generally unwell.

Before Parkinson's, I was an enthusiastic, reasonably skilled athlete. I played tennis as often as twice a day, I loved skiing, I rowed, I ran, I biked, and I hiked. Athletics was one of the ways I expressed my physical self in the world. At Tabor Academy in Marion, Massachusetts, where I attended boarding school, I lettered in three sports: football (as a cornerback), track, and crew. According to an old newspaper interview with my Tabor football coach, the late Jules Luchini, I had "cat-like quickness" and a keen ability to read plays that "rendered [me] a defensive stalwart." If Jules could only see me now!

At Cornell, I was too small for football, but I threw myself with enthusiasm into the lightweight crew, spending countless hours at the oars. All my adult life, until Parkinson's arrived, I ran competitively, often with my brother, George. I never felt quite as alive, nor did I ever have a better time than running road races with my brother or playing one of our countless one-on-one basketball games, even though my lifetime record against him is worse than my tennis record, for I never won a single basketball game, not a single, solitary one. What I wouldn't give to lose to George once again!

Being an athlete was always integral to my self-image. My self-confidence and my ego were all bolstered by physical activity and by my relative skill at most sports I tried. I moved with ease, and, at the risk of sounding immodest, a certain amount of grace. I was pleased with my physical presentation to the world, and athletics was part of it.

It wasn't just a personal pursuit. Sports was one of the ways we interacted as a family and was a very important part of our lives together. Caroline grew up on a surfboard in Southern California and was a talented skier. Penelope and Sarah, too, are excellent skiers and all-around athletes, lacrosse players at Cornell and Wesleyan respectively. My sons-in-law are both gifted athletes with whom I have spent countless hours in friendly competition. Vicki, too, is a fine tennis player, an excellent golfer, and an accomplished skier, as are her children. I have always been surrounded by, and attracted to, people who shared my passion and exhilaration for serious, sustained physical activity.

My inability now to share in these pursuits has taken away an important avenue of participation in the lives of my wife, my children and their families, my brother, and my stepchildren. No more road races with George, no more family ski trips, and no more basketball. And when I do "play" tennis, I know others are simply indulging me, because I am not even a shadow of the tennis player I once was.

* * *

The first change in my athletic life, an unrecognized harbinger of the Parkinson's to come, was the sudden inexplicable loss of my tennis serve several years ago. It was puzzling. The rest of my game was still solid, but coordinating the complex series of motions required for serving simply deserted me. Although I also had started to experience some of my early difficulties at work, I drew no connection between the two. And I still didn't make the connection when I started having periodic episodes of dizziness on the court. I had a remarkable ability to disregard all these early warning signs.

Later, on a Rocky Mountain ski slope in 2002, the winter after we were married, Vicki and I and all our kids (including my sons-in-law) had exited a ski lift at Vail where Penelope and Sarah had worked as ski instructors several years before. We were gathering together to begin our descent into one of Vail's luxuriously powdered bowls when I lost my balance and fell to the side. That alone wasn't alarming—an isolated momentary shift in weight that could have happened to anyone. But I simply could not muster the coordination to uncross my skis and get myself upright. I felt paralyzed. With the help of family, I managed to get up and ski down the hill without further incident, but my self-confidence had taken a serious hit. Was it age, or something more serious? I didn't know, and I started obsessing about it. Every future ski trip became fraught with anxiety. I soon found the entire production—getting the skis on the car, buying the lift tickets, and negotiating the lift lines—oddly confusing and difficult.

Always fearless on the slopes, I started worrying, for the first time, about hitting a tree or another skier. When I did ski after the fall in Vail, I kept thinking back to an incident the year before when I went to the rescue of a skier who had had a terrible collision with a tree. People were screaming, the snow was falling hard, and the skier went into cardiac arrest. When the ski patrol arrived, they had a laryngoscope but not a defibrillator, and I intubated the man on the spot. Despite my efforts, he was dead on arrival at the hospital.

The experience haunted me as my skill on skis went into a tailspin. I feared I would become the victim, not the rescuer. My confidence on the slopes, and my skiing itself, quickly deteriorated in a vicious cycle of doubt, loss of technique, and loss of physical confidence, yet I *still* didn't make the connection, perhaps because I didn't want to, between what was happening to me athletically and my increasing difficulties at work, or even my episodes of syncope and fainting.

Today, the physical prowess and athleticism that were so much a part of my life and my self-image are gone. But this isn't the only physical change that eats away at my self-confidence; it's also my physical appearance, which had always been a source of pride and an underpinning of my sense of self-worth. The way I present to the world has changed dramatically.

As I move through my ever-shrinking physical world, I have an acute self-consciousness that I never had before. The inner core of security I once had about my looks is under assault, because the entire architecture of my face and body has changed. Some mornings, I see acute disarray in the mirror. There are changes in the contours of my face, there is flattening of my skin tone, and there is a lack of affect (called *masked facies*) caused by an involuntary relaxation of tiny facial muscles that ordinarily keep the face animated and taut. It is a classic Parkinsonian look, to those familiar with the disease.

I used to see an attractive, well-put-together man in the mirror. There are still days when I glimpse that guy in my reflection, when I look, for a short time anyway, more like my old self than my Parkinson's self. But most days I see Parkinson's etched into my face. For a long time I was convinced that Parkinson's had given my head a pronounced egg shape, and I obsessed over it. Today that image has dissipated. Whether the image I saw ever existed, I don't know. Maybe it still does and I have just managed to muster the defense mechanisms to beat it back.

The changes that come with Parkinson's can be so subtle and slow to develop and progress that at times I'm not even sure if I perceive them any more or notice them as much as others do. And which changes are related to Parkinson's, as opposed to the normal changes that come with aging? It matters, because it would be much easier to accept natural changes that come with age. Those caused by Parkinson's terrify me, because I am obsessed and fearful about the progression of the disease and always alert for any changes that might signal an advance of the illness. Yet the disease and aging processes are so intertwined that there is often no way to tell.

The bottom line is that where I once took pride in my appearance, my physical presentation to the world now leaves a lot to be desired. The frequently inaudible voice; the hunkered-down, flat expression; the tremors and involuntary jerks of the hands and arms; the drippy nose; the sweats; the old man's stoop; the gaped, open mouth—I'm deeply embarrassed by it all. I detest the drooling and the dripping, the cramps, and the shuffling gait. There are days when trying to adjust to this reality is too much to take. I want the old me, the running back of my dream, back.

* * *

To try to offset the changes in my physical appearance, I make a point of always dressing well and trying to appear kempt, but even clothing has its challenges. Much as I try to monitor my clothing, my belt often misses a loop or two, my zipper may be at half-mast, and keeping food from making its mark is a regular challenge.

Not long ago, while Vicki was away on business, I went to a cocktail party. She made all the plans, part of her effort to keep me in the game, and arranged for a friend of ours to pick me up, take me to the party, and bring me back home.

Readying myself for an evening like this is now a major production. In addition to the anxiety about how well I will "perform," all the ordinary steps needed to get ready—shave, shower, dress—require inordinate effort. But by the time I was ready to go, the effort had paid off. I managed to look quite well put-together, or so I thought.

When the doorbell rang, the woman I was expecting to pick me up wasn't there. It was someone else; and though I should have recognized her, I didn't, and her name completely eluded me. It was as if I'd never seen her before, though she seemed vaguely familiar. So, off we went, with me trying desperately to figure out who I was with, but trying to mask my ignorance at the same time.

At the party, I talked with several people (intelligibly or not, I don't really know), had something to eat, and then went to find the bathroom. When I looked in the mirror, I saw that my tie, which I thought I had tied to perfection, was simply draped around my neck chaotically. Yet no one had said a thing all evening; they were, I suppose, trying to spare me the embarrassment. And that's exactly what I felt.

The minutes started to tick by as I did battle with my tie, and I began to get anxious that someone would knock on the bathroom door to see if I was all right because I had been gone for what seemed like a long time. I wasn't sure whether I had locked the door—unfamiliar locks are hard for me to figure out—so I started to fret that someone might just walk in. To tie my tie I had to take my jacket off; and the more anxious I got, the more pressure I felt to get the deed done; and the more pressure I felt, the more trouble I had with my tie.

This, like putting the lid on my coffee, is one of life's smallest, most trivial moments—the simple tying of a tie—and yet for me it became an ordeal. I was distraught because I thought I'd done the job at home, and now, as I tried to correct the problem, it was cascading into major anxiety and deep frustration. If this were an isolated incident, the anger would quickly pass, but this happens to me *all day long* as I try to go about the business of daily living. Every physical act has become a ten on the degree-of-difficulty scale. Consequently, my days are draped in a sense of unease. Is it any wonder that my self-confidence has taken a major hit?

The old Tom, the Harvard cardiologist, can't conduct a transaction at an ATM any more. I need the teller to total my checks and write out the deposit slip, because I can't do the math and my writing is illegible. Because they don't know why, the tellers sometimes assume I am lazy or stupid and look at me with thinly disguised contempt.

"Why don't you just tell them you have Parkinson's?" Vicki asks. It's a logical question. It's obvious just from looking at me that *something* is wrong. Who am I kidding by trying to hide it? Didn't I learn this lesson in the final months of my medical practice? If I explained, I would probably avoid the humiliating "what's wrong with this guy" stares I have grown accustomed to. The answer is that there is a lot of vanity involved. I don't want to be written off as a Parkinson's patient, even if my disarray *is* written all over my face and body.

The old Tom, the tennis player, now sometimes needs his personal trainer to tie his shoes and zip his sweatshirt. The old Tom, the football player, now has people offering to carry a bag, or to help him on with his coat. The old Tom, the skier, now needs help going down stairs.

The lack of physical control means I have to be very aware of all aspects of my environment for my own safety. All of us have to be aware of our surroundings to avoid physical harm, but for me the level of vigilance required to navigate the physical world safely is extraordinary. After I took several falls in the shower, we installed safety bars, a necessity for someone who needs three or four showers a day to cope with the extremes of hot and cold I experience. I can't open a wine bottle or push the right button in an elevator. If I have to avoid a falling object—a can falling from a high pantry shelf, for example—or if I get in the shower and find the water ice-cold or scalding, I don't have the agility or quickness to respond.

I have, in short, lost confidence in how my body will act or react at any given time. My anger about this loss of physical control sometimes threatens to overwhelm me. My life has become an endless series of small humiliations and compromises, each one a trifle on its own, but together enough to blow a big hole through my ego. But where once I resisted, I now accept help more gracefully. People want to help, need to help, and feel good about helping. But I wonder: Do you ever get used to not being able to tie your own shoes and button your own jacket?

This is one of the reasons I increasingly find myself most comfortable at home. Home is where I can avoid endless embarrassments and small humiliations. Home is where I can best control my environment. I know where everything is, how the faucets work (it will take exactly three turns of the shower handle to the left to get the water to the temperature I like) and the locks on the doors, too, so it is less effort to exist physically in this small world.

*　*　*

My sense of myself as a physical being isn't just affected by a lack of physical control; there is a flagging sense of wellness too. My vigor is gone. My fantasy—shared, I am sure, by all Parkinson's patients—is that there will be something, a magic elixir, to restore the sense of vigor, the miracle drug that will juice me up without side effects. While I occasionally string together two or three days when I feel great, days when I indulge myself in the fantasy that maybe it will go on like this forever, the fact is that most days, a sense of malaise, unease, and illness that can range from mild to severe overtakes me.

Some of it is the drugs. Parkinson's medications are a double-edged sword. On the one hand, they are my lifeline. Without the medications, I experience serious muscle aches and pains, cramping, and tension in the neck, upper body, and legs, all of which make it impossible to remain still (on airplane flights, I always try for an aisle seat so I can be up and moving when I need to). Without my meds, I feel washed-out, the tremors become uncontrollable, my gait deteriorates, and my body starts begging for heat. The downside, however, is that while the drugs stave off these symptoms, they bring on episodes of near narcolepsy and a general malaise. This is the paradox of the drugs—they can sometimes alleviate symptoms of malaise, and sometimes trigger them. Naps have become crucial to my functioning. When the malaise and pervasive fatigue descend and I seem out to lunch, a nap is restorative, indeed mandatory. Following a nap, I can have a few productive hours. Physical exercise, too, helps beat back the malaise.

* * *

I know I will never regain my tennis game, and that my skiing and running days may, at age sixty-three, be over. But the need to assert myself physically is a powerful one, even more so today than ever before. With all the compromises I have been forced to make because of my physical limitations, with the world I inhabit getting smaller and smaller, exercising as aggressively as I can has become an obsession. Seven days a week, I spin, practice yoga, or work out with a trainer. When I am seated safely on a spin bike, I feel a sense of control and well-being. A lot of people can't complete a one-hour spin class, so I take some pride that even with Parkinson's I can do what many others cannot. It bolsters my sagging ego. When I started spinning, I thought I might go once a month, but the sense of elation I get is so gratifying that I go three or four times a week.

Harder and less exhilarating, but just as important, are my

workouts with a personal trainer. Weight training is the focus, but we also work on kick-boxing, one of the most exhausting physical activities I've ever tried. I keep it up for three minutes, but I am ready to drop after thirty seconds. Is such a level of physical exertion wise for a man with a pacemaker and prone, because of the Parkinson's, to sudden hypotension? Despite the risks, reasserting my physical self through exercise has emotional and psychic rewards that are invaluable. In a world so circumscribed, rigorous exercise isn't a luxury, it's a necessity. Beyond the immediate high and sense of well-being that come with exercise, I believe it can and will slow my mental and physical decline. With a pacemaker and Parkinson's, in the back of my mind there is always the thought that I may be at increased risk of a cardiac event from vigorous exercise. But I will take that risk . . . every day.

For decades, I recommended exercise to patients as an effective way to reduce the medical risks of obesity, high cholesterol, and stress. It is quite common for the ill to fear that strenuous physical activity of any kind, be it exercise or sex, will cause them harm. This is especially true for patients with heart disease. As a result, their lives become increasingly limited, and depression follows. This, in turn, often contributes to further deterioration of their physical health.

Not too long ago, patients who had undergone heart surgery were instructed to take extended bed rest. Today such patients are urged to be up and moving as soon as possible. Inactivity, far from being restorative and therapeutic, was found to be a contributing factor to adverse outcomes, and I have no doubt that this was partly attributable to the psychological effects of inertia. As I confront life with Parkinson's and Lewy body disease, I have taken these lessons to heart. A body in motion will stay in motion.

When we speak of the mind-body connection, we most often think of the ways that the mind can affect the body. It has been understood for centuries that the mind exerts a powerful influence on the heart. In 1628, William Harvey wrote: "Every affectation of the mind that is attended with either pain or pleasure, hope or fear, is the cause of an agitation whose influence extends to the heart." Depression or stress, for example, is likely to manifest in other physical symptoms—weight loss or gain, an increase in blood pressure, fatigue, or heart palpitations. An older patient who has lost a spouse is at higher risk of a cardiac event because grief and loneliness burden the heart. Similarly, laughter, intimacy, and joy can ease the burden on the heart. Many nontraditional, or so-called "complementary," therapies are based on the premise that the mind can help heal the body, and the placebo effect in medicine is all about the mind's influence over the body.

We think less often about the body's effect on the mind. The deterioration of physical skills, the loss of control over one's body, and the physical symptoms of an illness such as Parkinson's have profound effects on the mind and the spirit. Physical illness can be the catalyst for a cascading deleterious loop in which physical symptoms lead to depression, stress, anger, anxiety, and isolation—which, in turn, cause further physical deterioration. Breaking this vicious cycle—throwing a monkey wrench into these works—is what my daily exercise is all about. It's a struggle to stay positive, engaged, and active, but I am holding my own.

* * *

As my physical abilities have deteriorated, I think of my father. Later in his life, after suffering multiple strokes, he went every day to his office in Providence, Rhode Island. He was obese and couldn't really work any more, so he sat at his desk and read the paper and drank coffee. That image motivates me to push through and to keep my body in motion, always in motion.

* * *

Parkinson's in older patients is typically accompanied by co-morbid diseases that complicate life, whether it's diabetes, heart disease, or cancer. Many of these patients are already slowed by old age. But Parkinson's for the relatively young, like me, strikes people in the prime of life and at the pinnacle of their careers.

Oddly enough, despite the litany of symptoms that match those commonly found in the very elderly—poor vision, lack of balance, lack of vigor, memory loss, sexual dysfunction, malaise, and so on—I don't feel old or perceive myself as old. Maybe it's because I don't look my age, despite the physical changes Parkinson's has wrought. Maybe it's spending time with younger, active people—children, grandchildren, and even my fellow spinners—that keeps me feeling younger. And maybe it's the power of mind over body and body over mind. I refuse, despite the burden of my disease, to give in to old age prematurely.

Never underestimate the power of positive thinking, or of simple exercise, to help you get up off the mat. I will never break through the line and score that touchdown I dreamed about, but I will, as long as I possibly can, keep taking the ball and pushing it a few yards down the field.

EIGHT
End Game

SOME THIRTY-ODD YEARS ago, I read a story in *The New Yorker* about a Princeton-educated physician with Alzheimer's who walked into the waves off Nantucket Island and drowned. It was not an accident. But the drowning was not a demented or deranged act. The doctor was, in his own way, following an ancient Eskimo custom without the ice. He knew his dementia was progressing, and he didn't want to live his life unable to recognize his family, unable to take care of himself, and housed, perhaps, in a facility surrounded by equally demented, hollowed-out souls. I think a lot about that doctor these days—I can still vividly recall the photograph that accompanied the article—as I play out in my mind the many different scenarios that could unfold as my dementia progresses.

"Progression" has become the most terrifying word in the English language for me. In the year that it has taken to write this book, my lapses have become more frequent, my ability to express myself more compromised, my intellectual capital a little more depleted. The progression is slow but noticeable. The tiny pieces of everyday existence that are becoming more elusive and more difficult to navigate, are translated into a general unhappiness and sense of foreboding about further losing control.

Will I lose myself, my very essence, to this disease? It's the question that dogs me day in and day out. So I am evaluating myself all the time. Am I getting worse? If so, how significant are the changes? Over what period of time have they occurred? Is the ratio of bad days to good increasing?

In its most primitive form, I experience dementia as a cessation of thought accompanied by a desperate attempt to regain control of my thought process. I rely on phrases like "it's coming" or "hang on" to break the awkward silences and to signal that I am aware of what is happening. Though I still have enough wits to sense that my dementia is progressing, others provide the reality check, the feedback that allows for a more objective assessment. If I ask Vicki or my daughters if I seem worse, they usually respond by saying there are changes, but they are subtle and minor. This is the "politically correct" response, designed not to feed my rampant anxieties, so naturally I distrust it. But I cling to the hope that I will fall into that lucky category of people who will face a very slow progression that would give me at least twenty more years of decent quality-of-life.

* * *

But I fear losing control of my basic bodily functions, being unable to recognize my daughters (the heartbreak on their faces when I no longer know them is the most painful image of all), and coming to the day when my grandchildren are reluctantly urged by their parents to talk to their unresponsive grandfather. Such an experience, if it comes to pass, will remain with them all their lives. I want all of us to be spared this. The disease is fraying my communication with those I love, the connections scratchy with interference caused by the Lewy bodies. I mourn what's already been lost and fear the losses still to come, wondering if and when the connection, like a phone line gone down in a storm, will sever the bond forever.

* * *

At the end of their lives, both my parents suffered from dementia. Even when he was confined to a wheelchair following his stroke, a stroke that left him progressively demented, my father put on a suit and tie every day. When I would call home from Texas (I was in the Air Force then), my mother would always, at some point during our conversation, say to my dad, "It's your son Tommy. He wants to talk to you." It was a charade—my father barely knew who I was—but the charade allowed my mother a connection to a better past, when my father's mind had been intact. On visits home during leave from the Air Force, I would sometimes find my father sitting in his chair, reading the newspaper upside down. One day, as I went to take his blood pressure, I took his hand and noticed feces under his fingernails. It was devastating because he had no idea. His caretaker—a male aide who lived with him for a year—was equally oblivious. Always the most fastidious of people, my father had lost something essential to who he was.

In my mother's later years she always looked as attractive as ever, and she dressed to the nines every day. She could still sing and play the piano beautifully, but she didn't know me from Adam. When my mother needed more care than we—my brother and sister and I—could provide ourselves, we went to visit a Boston-area nursing home that specialized in caring for Alzheimer's patients. (Though we don't like to admit it, placing the demented in a nursing home or other strange environment will usually hasten their demise. That's not *why* people place their loved ones in nursing homes, but that is often the outcome.)

The staff took great pride in the facility, but it horrified me. The home operated on the principle that patients, at least those who were able-bodied and not a threat to others, should be allowed to wander throughout the facility and not be confined to their rooms. So, on the first floor, we saw all these aimless, vacant souls walking without a destination (in the literal and figurative sense). On the floor where patients with more advanced disease resided, those who were expected to die within months, the smell of urine was unmistakable. And this was one of the most respected and expensive homes of its kind in the area.

In the end, my mother remained at home with twenty-four-hour care.

I have seen one possible future and I want no part of it. I don't want to live if I have to live as my mother or father did at the end; and I would rather my money educate my grandchildren than be used for the care and upkeep of my body.

* * *

What will become of me?

There are more scenarios than I can keep track of, and no easy or obvious answers. I could develop another life-threatening illness, where decisions to treat or withhold medical care could be complicated by my dementia. It is generally accepted in the medical community that a person with advanced dementia will not, for example, receive an artificial heart or a kidney transplant. But what about a moderately demented person? Should a patient with advanced dementia have coronary bypass surgery or dialysis? Though few Parkinson's patients die from it, Lewy body disease changes that equation in unknown ways and could, itself, become life-threatening.

Or I could remain physically healthy but become so demented that I could not care for myself or even know who I am. I could lose the ability to communicate, but be more intact inside than anyone on the outside would know. My dementia could stop, at least for a while, somewhere between here and there, but render me difficult or impossible to care for at home, at least not without exacting a devastating emotional and financial toll from my family. The rate and severity of progression, my overall health, the potential toll on possible caretakers, the cost, the promise of new, still undiscovered treatments—these are just some of the factors that complicate planning for an unknowable future.

When Caroline was ill with cancer, we knew, more or less, how the disease would progress and that death was a relatively near-term certainty. But I have an illness in which physical death is not necessarily the endpoint. Mine could be a long, drawn-out process with no distinct ending. I could linger in the shadows of dementia for many years.

What I would want for myself in these different scenarios may not be what my daughters would want or could accept. For the moment, they have vowed to care for me indefinitely at home, come hell or high water. What Vicki may think is best may be at odds with what Penelope and Sarah want. I know firsthand how the caretaker's stock of emotional and physical energy can be depleted. My daughters are young, with husbands and small children to care for. No matter how much they protest that they will take care of me if Vicki cannot, their

energy level will flag at some point, and they will get worn
down emotionally and physically. Do I want them depleting
their reservoirs on me, when I may not even know who they
are? I would rather see that time and energy go to their growing families. It is pro forma for the ill to express the desire not
to be a burden, but I have seen enough serious illness in my life,
as a son, a husband, and a physician, to say, "But I *really* don't
want to be a burden."

⋆ ⋆ ⋆

Even as I am losing control over my mind and body, I can still,
today, exercise some control over my future by expressing my
wishes to my family. But how do I articulate those wishes when
the possible scenarios are so varied, when ambiguity rather than
clarity, subjectivity rather than objectivity, hope and dread attend
almost every aspect of the dilemma? Who is to say how much
dementia is too much to live with? Who will know what really
goes on in my head when I lose the ability to communicate? And,
assuming that all the members of my family and I come to a clear
understanding of the point of no return, how exactly—both medically and legally—does one go about ending a life when the body
is intact but the mind is gone? If I ask others to help me hasten
the end, will I be putting on their shoulders an unbearable burden? And if they shoulder that burden and act according to my
wishes, will I be sentencing them to a lifetime of guilt and doubt,
especially if they are uncomfortable with the decision?

No matter what decisions I make now about my future care,
no matter how precisely I try to outline what I would want done

under different sets of circumstances, events may unfold in ways that I cannot now foresee. So, at times, my thoughts turn back to that doctor on Nantucket. At least such an exit would spare others the excruciating life-and-death decisions. But such a scenario is also filled with uncertainty. If I decided, literally or figuratively, to walk into the waters off Nantucket, would I be able to make a rational decision at the right time? How will I know when the time is right? And, if I wait too long, do I risk the most unacceptable outcome of all—becoming a living but empty vessel?

Hospitalized patients with terminal diseases sometimes have their passage eased by sympathetic doctors under the guise of making the patient more comfortable, regardless of whether assisted suicide is legal. I have done that myself on very rare occasions, when my patients were already close to death and their suffering had become pointless. But what if I am of unsound mind but still sound of body, at the point where I can say emphatically today that I would not wish to go on? You cannot check into a hospital seeking to hasten death. You cannot enlist a friend or colleague in the process without exposing them to enormous legal risk.

Yet I think a lot about assisted suicide these days. But I also wonder whether such an exit is selfish. If my physical presence in this world, even when my mind is beyond reach, is meaningful for my daughters, how much weight should I accord to that? I am not afraid of dying; I am afraid of living with a mind that has been erased. I see no point in existing as a piece of cellular protoplasm. If I had a date certain for my death, I wouldn't be terrified of the future any more. Because what I fear isn't the end, but being in such a demented state that I no longer experience fear or joy—or anything else, for that matter. But talking and thinking about it is not the same as taking the fateful step. And what makes such a decision so profoundly wrenching is that it is utterly and irretrievably irrevocable. As I mull over these most difficult questions, I keep in mind some well-known words that Caroline found comforting as her days came to an end— and in which I, too, find solace:

Death is nothing at all
I have only slipped away into the next room
I am I and you are you
Whatever we were to each other
That we are still
Call me by my old familiar name
Speak to me in the easy way you always used
Put no difference into your tone
Wear no forced air of solemnity or sorrow
Laugh as we always laughed
At the little jokes we always enjoyed together
Play, smile, think of me, pray for me
Let my name be ever the household word that it always was
Let it be spoken without effort
Without the ghost of a shadow in it
Life means all that it ever meant
It is the same as it ever was
There is absolute unbroken continuity
What is death but a negligible accident?
Why should I be out of mind
Because I am out of sight?
I am waiting for you for an interval

Somewhere very near
Just around the corner
All is well.

Nothing is past; nothing is lost
One brief moment and all will be as it was before
How we shall laugh at the trouble of parting when we meet again!

HENRY SCOTT-HOLLAND, 1847–1918,
CANON OF ST. PAUL'S CATHEDRAL

Today, I have no easy conclusions to share, other than my wish to die at home and to have as peaceful a departure as possible. But no definitive decisions have been reached. What I *do* know is what I don't want, even if I don't yet know how to avoid it.

* * *

I have seen and experienced for myself the relief and release that follows the death of a person held very dear. There is no shame in that. Death is, in some ways, the grievously ill person's gift to the living. It is what releases the survivors from the gloomy twilight of debilitating illness, back into life.

I once had a patient, Mrs. E, whose husband always accompanied her, as I encouraged him to do, to her annual checkups. Mr. E was about eighty and was always impeccably dressed, animated, and handsome. During one meeting, Mrs. E asked if she could speak with me privately. Mr. E bounced up, said, "Of course," and left the room. Mrs. E shared with me deep concerns about Mr. E's behavior: He was on the path to dementia. I recommended a neurological evaluation, but Mrs. E and her adult children were afraid to even suggest to him that he might have Alzheimer's.

When I next saw the Es, he was still as dapper as ever, but he had refused the testing that his family had finally summoned up the courage to suggest. In the meantime, he had grown irascible and irritable and impossible for Mrs. E to manage at home. He was only in a nursing home for a few months before he died of pneumonia, a death that brought a combination of grief and incredible relief to his family.

I had similar feelings during Caroline's illness. The demands of caring for Caroline toward the end of her life were exhausting, emotionally and physically. I loved her, desperately wanted her to live, and feared her death. Just moments after she died—when the familiar tap of her cane on the floor went silent—Sarah, Penelope, and I lay on the couch paralyzed with fatigue. Into the enormous vacuum left by her absence rushed a flood of grief and relief.

Though I sometimes fear that the burden of caring for me will be too much for my daughters, who need to devote their energies to their own families, I sometimes fear the opposite— that they will have too much energy and keep me here longer than I would want to be around, postponing the relief and release that my death will bring to us all.

Though it is natural and normal to feel relief when a loved one suffering through a terrible illness dies, it does not make it any easier to make the difficult decisions that surround end-of-life care. Because death is so final, family members are terrified that they may give up early and be burdened with a lifetime of guilt, that the next day might bring some unexpected hope or miraculous recovery, though such instances are of course extraordinarily rare. But the fact that they do occur once in a blue moon plants seeds of doubt that make many family members hesitate, often only to prolong the suffering of their loved one and themselves. We feel that there is no room for error, yet errors are a part of medicine and of life.

In his book *How Doctors Think,* Harvard's Dr. Jerome Groopman writes about the biases and assumptions that can often lead a doctor down the path to an incorrect diagnosis. All physicians, even the best, probably have a story like Mr. H's that proves Dr. Groopman's case.

Mr. H was a longtime patient of mine, a man in his midseventies with a supportive family, some of whom were also my patients. One day I received a call from his family. He was physically fine, but was becoming very forgetful, and his forgetfulness seemed to have come on quickly. I made an assumption based on statistics (Alzheimer's among men in Mr. H's age group is very common) and my own predisposition (a lifelong fear of Alzheimer's). After meeting with Mr. H, I told the family I thought he had Alzheimer's and arranged for him to see a neurologist. But before we could even get Mr. H to a neurologist, he had a sudden and acute acceleration of his Alzheimer's symptoms and could no longer recognize his family.

Upon examination by the neurologist, it turned out that Mr. H was not suffering from Alzheimer's or an organic dementia at all. He had something that I had never even considered: normal pressure hydrocephalus, an obstruction in the brain that was causing fluid to collect in the brain casing. The pressure was relieved with a simple procedure, and the dementia-like symptoms disappeared immediately. The family thought I was brilliant for recommending the neurologist, even though I had been way off the diagnostic mark.

Thus, for doctors, caregivers, and family, making life-and-death decisions is fraught with anxiety about making incorrect assumptions and making irrevocable decisions based on them. Yet in my experience, far more often than not, caring families (as mine is) make excellent and fully appropriate decisions, even under the most painful and difficult circumstances.

In my case, how will we ever know that there won't be a sudden and dramatic reversal of the disease process, or that at some unknown date in the future a cure won't be found? Do I stay alive, even in a completely demented state with all that that would mean for my family and myself, hoping for those faint possibilities?

Eventually, I come to this question: When I no longer recognize them and my grandchildren, will my family, as an ultimate expression of their love, help me find an exit with grace and dignity?

* * *

In late May 2007, Penelope, Sarah, Vicki, and I sat down together with Susan Block for the first in what we expect will be a series of meetings to work through the complex issues surrounding my illness, including end of life. Despite the wish for clarity, most people with serious illness and their families muddle through such issues because there are so many unknowns. We, too, will be muddling through these issues, but we are hoping that regular meetings mediated by Susan will help us through the process with minimum damage to the family relationships and maximum honesty.

Though I used this first meeting to state my general wish that I not live when I am too demented to know my own family, no specific plan of action, no specific guidelines or markers, were laid down. And as I learned just a week later in a slightly different context, the clarity one reaches on such issues can go right out the window when the time comes to make real life-and-death decisions.

The irony was inescapable, but just a week after this first meeting, I found Bozeman, the golden retriever who lay by Caroline's bed during the final weeks of her illness, the dog who still connected me to her, unresponsive in our house. Late that night, Vicki and I were at Angel Memorial Hospital, the preeminent veterinary hospital in Boston, trying to decide what to do. Bozeman is thirteen years old, and the nature of his ailment was not yet clear. Did it make sense to subject him to various tests? Exploratory surgery? And, at his advanced age, did it make sense to try to save him? As we wrestled with these questions, the obvious parallels to the discussion we had just had about the possible end-of-life care for me were unspoken but very much present. My immediate instinct was to bring Bozeman home and make him as comfortable as possible. Vicki, and the next day Sarah, argued for the non-invasive ultrasound the veterinarian suggested as an option, to see if an abdominal mass might be present. (It was. Bozeman has an inoperable tumor on his spleen.)

But what became immediately clear to me is that no matter how much we intellectualize and plan for the day when a critical life-and-death decision will have to be made, when that day comes all bets are off. There will be nuanced options, emotions will be unpredictable, and any clarity achieved months earlier will dissipate. Muddling through may be the only real option, no matter how hard we try today to plan for my life tomorrow.

NINE

A Life Beyond Illness

RANDOLPH ("RY") RYAN was a Pultizer Prize–winning journalist with the *Boston Globe* who became a patient of mine more than two decades ago, and, in the years that followed, a close and dear friend. A man of towering intellect, Ry was a man of great passion—for people, for ideas, and for good causes—and he was an adventurer. He also suffered from atrial fibrillation, a generally benign and treatable heart rhythm problem, and, under my care, Ry did very well. I always told him to be sure to report any changes he felt, especially any chest pain, as soon as possible.

Over the New Year's holiday a few years ago, I was away on vacation when I received a call telling me Ry was dead, of a heart attack, at the age of sixty-one. I was shocked and nearly catatonic with grief. He died without warning, or so I thought. Eerily, when I returned home there was a voice-mail message Ry had left a few days before. He called to wish me a happy New Year, to say we should get together soon and, by the way, he was having a little bit of chest discomfort so perhaps he should come in for a checkup.

Like most physicians, I cannot recall every patient I have ever seen over many years of practice, especially those who have done well. But I never forget those who have not. I agonized over Ry's death, not just because he was a close friend whom I deeply admired, but because I was his doctor. When I spoke with his wife shortly after his death, she told me she wasn't even aware that he was having any chest pain; he simply went into cardiac arrest.

To this day, I wonder: Did I make it sufficiently clear, did I impress upon him enough, the need to be vigilant at the first sign of symptoms? Did I miss something in my diagnosis? Had I unwittingly contributed to his early death? If I had been home for the holiday and heard his phone message sooner, might he be alive today? I anguished over Ry's death for months. Thoughts of what might have been, could have been, and should have been played over and over in my mind.

Ry's story, which I had buried for several years, surfaced again when I was close to completing work on this book. At first I wasn't sure why—or how, if at all—it was connected to the story of my own illness. Then it dawned on me: The questions that plagued me about Ry were the very same unanswerable questions that plagued me about Caroline's illness and now my own.

Despite all my skill and knowledge as a physician, I could not cure Ry's illness or Caroline's, nor could I prevent their deaths. I lost control of their health and their lives—if, indeed, they had ever been mine *to* control. Likewise, I wasn't able to prevent myself from becoming ill. I mull over all the questions I asked myself about Ry and Caroline with respect to myself: Is there something I could have done to keep myself healthy? Was it the grief over Caroline and the intense stress of her illness that somehow triggered my Parkinson's? Did I miss something that would have prevented my illness or lessened its severity? Was I sufficiently vigilant? For most people, living with serious illness means wrestling with similar, unanswerable questions, pondering an unknowable future, accepting the unacceptable and, at times, thinking the unthinkable. You have to discipline yourself to put those questions aside at times, or they will consume you in a vicious cycle of self-pity and remorse.

* * *

Parkinson's and Lewy body disease have taken much of the density, richness, and texture from my life, and moved much that was once within my grasp to a place beyond my control. However, between the limbo of illness and the anger and despair it often spawns, there is a better place—a life beyond illness still to be lived.

* * *

As Sir William Osler, one of the icons of modern medicine, noted early in the twentieth century, no two people are ill in exactly the same way. There are, therefore, no simple prescriptions for moving beyond illness. Shaped by countless genetic and environmental forces, some people have enormous reservoirs of optimism, while others are predisposed to despair. Some are by nature proactive, while others are passive. We have different tolerances for pain, physical and emotional, and different temperaments. As I have said, a patient's pre-morbid personality will dictate much about how they traverse the landscape of their illness.

As a physician, I had to take all of these differences into account when offering words of advice and comfort to patients and determining how best to treat them. The approach was not always the same, even for those patients with nearly identical medical conditions. One size does not fit all when it comes to nurturing in patients a sense of hope and optimism about the future. Here, however, I can only offer general advice, some ideas that are simple and practical on the surface but not always easy to put into practice, and some that are more philosophical. My hope is that there will be some comfort in these thoughts for everyone living with Parkinson's or dementia—or any serious illness, for that matter—either as patient, family member, or friend. If you or someone you know has been diagnosed with Parkinson's or dementia in any of its forms, you have taken a serious blow. There is no minimizing the challenges that lie ahead. There will be plenty of anguish, anger, and heartache. But the question is, do you fold your tent and surrender to the disease, or do you push hard to reach the outer limits of what is possible? Will you allow the illness to control you, or will you assert yourself to gain some control over your illness? Do you succumb to despair, or do you find ways to extract pleasure from life, despite the limitations illness imposes? Yes, much has been and will be lost, but much remains, and there is a life to be lived. How?

* * *

Serious illness is a struggle on many levels, but it is, in no small measure, a search for hope and courage: hope that things will get better, and the courage to move forward even if they don't. Your doctors, family, and friends can be of enormous help in this search, but ultimately hope and courage come from within. Locating the wellspring of hope and courage in any individual is not always an easy task, but I never cease to be amazed at how many patients with serious illness discover a resolve, an inner strength, and a will to persevere that surprises even them.

Though I part company politically with Senator John McCain, in my own dark moments I draw inspiration from his remarkable story of human resilience. During six years in solitary confinement as a prisoner of war in North Vietnam, enduring the most horrible conditions, McCain survived on hope in what was a nearly hopeless situation. He and his fellow POWs in nearby cells developed a code of their own that allowed them to tap messages to one another on the walls, testimony to the power of human contact to sustain us through dark hours. But in the end, McCain and his fellow POWs survived on nothing except a thin reed of hope that someday, somehow, they would come home. In hope they discovered courage. The same lesson applies in medicine. As Jerome Groopman has written, "Hope gives us the courage to confront our circumstances and the capacity to surmount them."

When hope is lost, there is only despair. But for Parkinson's patients, and those with dementia, there are two kinds of hope.

In the spring of 2007, I began taking a new medication, Namenda (new to me, but not to the pharmacopeia). Indicated for moderate to severe dementia, the drug generally does not perform well when used alone. However, in combination with Aricept, commonly used to treat Alzheimer's, it can, I am discovering, be very helpful indeed. At least for now. I feel better, I think better, and I speak better; and, not surprisingly, my mood has brightened as a result.

In late May 2007, the Fuller Museum in Brockton, Massachusetts, where Caroline was once the director, hosted a benefit to support a fund named in her honor. For the first time in recent memory, I spoke extemporaneously about Caroline, her service to the museum, and what the museum meant to her. I was articulate and relaxed. There was no sweating, no moments of disorientation. I was completely buoyed by the experience and felt the return of the social confidence I had long ago lost. How long this good run will continue is unknowable—weeks, months, years—but for now I am greatly encouraged. Thanks to the new medications, I feel as if my disease is in a remission. This is, of course, the wish of every patient with Parkinson's or dementia—that medical science will justify our hopes. Parkinson's and Lewy body disease progress over many years, so there is always hope that new research will lead to new treatments in the not-too-distant future.

Public awareness of Parkinson's has increased dramatically in recent years. Michael J. Fox has given Parkinson's a very public face, and his foundation has raised millions of dollars to explore new treatments for the disease. And as dementia in its various forms afflicts more and more Americans, many of them still quite young, we are seeing a huge upsurge in media attention to this growing public health challenge. This new public focus is likely to accelerate research in the field. New technologies hold promise that diseases such as Alzheimer's and other forms of dementia may be detectable before symptoms appear, which, in turn, may lead to medical and pharmacological strategies to prevent, delay onset, or mitigate symptoms.

This is the hope of science, and it is not a chimera. Of course, for those of us deep in the throes of our disease, such hopes cannot be realized too soon, and some of us may never have the promise of science fulfilled in our lifetimes. But hope exists not just in a cure or new treatments that alleviate symptoms; it lives within.

* * *

I don't have a simple prescription that will help you or someone you love live your life beyond illness, or tell you how to tap the hope that lives within. The best I can do is to tell you my story, how I have coped and tried—sometimes successfully, sometimes not—to rise above illness. By giving voice to the experience, I hope to encourage and provide a modicum of comfort.

If you were my patient, however, I would draw you near and say this: Use your family and friends as motivation to live life with as much grace as you can muster. We are accountable to our families for how we conduct ourselves through our illness. Be honest with yourself and your family about how you feel, but recognize that it is within your power to lighten their burden—not with false assurances and unconvincing cheeriness, but by living as fully as possible within the space allowed by your illness. That space may be larger than you think. Being aggressive about being well—staying active through whatever avenues are open to you—will help decompress your family's anxiety. I often use my grandchildren as motivation to assert as much control as I can over my illness. I can't be everything I wanted to be to them, but they are part of the why and wherefore of my existence, and I am determined to be as much as I can of the grandfather that I wanted to be.

Find a safe place, a therapist's office or a dear friend's living room, to unburden yourself of anger. There is often a lot of misdirected anger in illness. Don't allow your anger at God, or at fate, to spill over onto those who love you and can help you. Be deserving of their love and compassion and their desire to help.

You will mourn the old, healthy you, but if you have an irreversible or progressive disease as I do, life will be better if you accept your new reality. Acceptance is key to defusing anger, stress, and self-pity. If you measure the quality of your days today by the days you had when you were healthy, you will always find them wanting. Your challenge now is to make the most of your days by a new standard and to find new pleasures within whatever boundaries your illness imposes.

If you are able-bodied, exercise, whether it's walking or something more rigorous, because it will improve your sense of well-being. If you cannot exercise physically, exercise your mind. Read the paper, keep up on the news of the world, and discuss it with friends and family. It always helps to realize that the world is bigger than your illness.

Use your faith in God, if you believe in God. There were times when Caroline was ill when, for no apparent reason, I would sit in the non-denominational chapel at the Brigham and Women's Hospital, even though I am not a religious person. Yet sometimes I would find comfort in prayer. It was a place where I could be alone with my thoughts. But typically, when I was in acute psychic pain, I would go running. On the road, no one could reach me, and I would find myself asking: Do I have faith? If so, in whom? In what? Organized religion can give, to those who believe, access to a belief system that is a touchstone, a constant, that can ease much of the angst of those unanswerable questions that are part and parcel of serious illness. And being part of a community, religious or otherwise, can be a source of strength, comfort, and tranquility. Whether we are religious in the traditional sense, or simply spiritual, we all search for explanations for our illness. In my experience, most patients find it harder to accept serious illness as a random occurrence than as part of a larger plan, because the loss of control that comes with being ill is that much more painful.

But, whether you believe your illness is part of God's plan or not, you should have a plan of your own: a plan to manage your illness, and a life plan too. Finding purpose, even in a life circumscribed by illness, is essential.

When I saw patients for the first time, after taking a detailed medical history, running tests, and making a diagnosis, I was usually able to begin our post-diagnosis discussion by saying, "Your problem is one we have seen before and dealt with successfully in the past. There is every reason to expect that you will do well." And then I would take out a pad of paper and say to the patient, "Now, together we are going to write out our plan for managing your case."

In longhand (I *never* gave the patient a photocopy of instructions), I would write out the medications I was recommending and what they were for. I would ask the patient what he or she thought was a reasonable exercise regimen within their abilities, and I'd write that into the plan as well. We'd discuss dietary and other lifestyle changes that would help the patient do well, and I wrote those down too. Even if I had written a hundred nearly identical plans in the past, the act of handwriting each patient's plan was essential to its efficacy: It was the "contract" between me and the patient that, if adhered to, would help ensure a positive outcome. And because the plan was *personal* to each patient, it was more likely to be honored. Just leaving the office with that handwritten plan in hand inspired hope, because implicit in that plan was the message that there were things the patient could do to take control of their illness. Indeed, while there may have been three hundred words on that page, it really was just one: "hope." The written plan inspired hope that by following the instructions on the paper, things would get better. At the bottom of the plan I wrote my home phone number, and some patients carried it with them for decades. Why? Because it provided a sense of security and allayed their anxiety. It conveyed that I would be a partner in carrying out the plan. Giving out my home phone number was, in a word, therapeutic.

Patients confronting chronic illness should make a plan, too, if they are able. The plan should include those steps needed to manage the illness itself (medications, lifestyle changes, doctor's instructions), but it should also be a plan for living. Write down all the things you wanted to do in life (or want to do now) but didn't have the chance to do—visit the Great Barrier Reef, learn a language or how to play bridge, *write a book,* read the classics— and do at least some of those that are still within your grasp. (My own list includes a course in creative writing; studying Spanish; learning more about physics, which always eluded me in college; "shadowing" my daughter Sarah, now an equine veterinarian, and learning more about veterinary medicine; and counseling other Parkinson's patients.) If you can volunteer somewhere, do it. Find something that gives you pleasure and makes you feel useful and involved. I realize that for some, illness is so debilitating, or dementia can be so severe, that this is not possible; but I also know that too many people give up too early, and their downward arc becomes a self-fulfilling prophesy.

It takes great self-discipline to be proactive when illness can be so diminishing, and it requires the support of those around you. If you don't want others—your family, friends, and caretakers—to give up on you, you cannot give up on yourself. With a disease that is robbing me of control, asserting whatever control I can over my external environment helps tame the internal furies. Diet, exercise, socializing with those I most care about—taking control of what I *can* control—gives me a certain level of peace. And in doing so, I signal to those around me that I have not given up on myself. Proactive patients fare better than those who are passive. Even when you have lost so much of the density of your life, as I have, piece together a life from the things you still can do and enjoy. For me, I can still communicate, albeit not nearly as well as before. I can counsel other Parkinson's patients, I can still be physically active, I cherish my grandchildren, and I love my wife, music, and movies: Build a life from the blocks that are left.

Depending on the illness, you may, as I do, have days when you think the diagnosis must be wrong because you feel so good. The new drug I am on is, as of this writing, giving me great cause for optimism that my symptoms can be managed; some days I feel absolutely terrific. But, even as I enjoy my improved intellectual functioning on Namenda, I have been having more frequent disconcerting episodes of sudden hypotension that cause near-collapse, a sign that the Lewy body disease is becoming more diffuse throughout my brain. Be prepared for the emotional roller coaster that comes with the one step forward and one step back that is so common in serious illness. There will be good days and bad, times of progress and regression, signs of encouragement and discouragement. Expect that in such sequences you may feel rebound anger, because the feeling on the upside can be seductive. You may think you have turned a corner, only to have your disease pull you back face-to-face with reality.

Every day Vicki and I have moments of pain and sorrow, many of them around my inability to perform some trivial activity of daily living. But we try to inject some levity into it so it doesn't consume us. As you trundle down this path, you need a release for your anger, and humor is often powerful medicine.

I hate grocery shopping, but occasionally we end up at the market together—when we are returning from spinning, for example. On one such recent occasion, I found myself growing irritable with Vicki because the shopping trip was dragging on and on ("We only need a few items," she had promised) and I was eager to get home. I started looking at my watch. At one point, in full pique, I said to Vicki that I was going to take the groceries we had, go through the checkout line myself, and go home. After a very brief but tense standoff, we simultaneously realized the absurdity of my threat: The only car we had with us was hers, she had the only key, and, in any event, in my current state I can't drive her car—it's too big and too intimidating for me. Besides, given how long it would take me to navigate the checkout line and get the groceries to the car, I wasn't likely to cut the trip any shorter anyway, even if I could have driven her car. I wasn't going anywhere until Vicki was good and ready to leave. Our moment of simultaneous realization brought laughter and immediate release from the building tension.

* * *

In his Holocaust memoir, *Man's Search for Ultimate Meaning,* Dr. Viktor Frankl wrote: "Those who know how close the connection is between the state of mind of a man—and his courage and hope, or lack of them—and the state of immunity of his body will understand that the sudden loss of hope and courage can have a deadly effect."

In my practice, I often wrote small notes that I gave to patients as they left my office. To demonstrate my faith in their future, I might write, "When I see you in a year, we may be able to take you off one of your medications. Show me this note next year as a reminder." This simple act signaled my expectation that the patient, perhaps fearful of sudden cardiac death, would be in my office a year hence. One patient, a physician named Dr. H with serious heart disease, told me of his deep remorse that he might not be alive for his daughter's wedding a few months hence. To him I wrote, "You will dance at your daughter's wedding. Show me this note at our next meeting." Dr. H did dance at his daughter's wedding and proudly pulled the note out of his pocket at his next appointment. He lived for a few more years. Did these notes, often kept close by in wallets and jacket pockets, stave off death? No, but I believe the hope they inspired absolutely prolonged the lives of many a patient.

It is one thing to try to inspire hope and courage in the ill. I know from personal experience, as both a physician and patient, that it can be quite another for the patient to find it.

In the waning days of her life, Caroline, though well aware she was dying, nevertheless found hope and courage. She found it in me, in our daughters, in countless devoted friends, and in her faith. A few months before she died, she penned a short poem intended as a thank-you to all those who took up her struggle as their own. The opening line is a reference to the chemotherapy drip to which she was attached when she wrote the poem; the "Reservoir" refers to one of her favorite places to walk when she was still able. The poem, printed in the small program distributed at her funeral, reflects her courage and hope, and inspires the same in me. It is fitting that I give my dear Caroline the last word:

In a port above my heart
chemistry streams
Transforming the embattled universe
in which I live. In the arms of your attention
I am safely carried,
closely held. At night,
waking in the Valley of the shadow
I call out to you
Who walk with me beside the Reservoir.
You, who bring me soups and sweaters.
You who call and praise and
Laugh and counsel
Fill me. I need nothing more.

Acknowledgments

I am deeply indebted to the many individuals who assisted me with this project and I would like to acknowledge their support and dedication.

My devoted family:

Vicki Tenney Graboys, my wife, an amazing woman who is multi-talented and consistently works 24/7. Vicki didn't fully understand her role when she "signed on the line." But she has adjusted to this reality, watches me like a hawk, is committed to my well-being, and effects for me as stress free an environment as possible. I am blessed to have her in my life.

Special appreciation to my daughters, Sarah and Penelope, who were always "watching my back" and have always expressed unconditional love. I am blessed once again.

My two sons-in-law, Patrick Blair and Thomas Valeo. I could not have wished for kinder, more decent husbands for my daughters. Much appreciation to my step-children, Jennifer Baker Hinton, Carson Baker, and Olivia Baker. Without their support this project might not have come to fruition.

George Graboys—patriarch of the clan; there are no words to express his devotion and my appreciation.

William Rigby and Nikila Ellis—my brother-in-law and sister-in-law. They were the "go to" persons and confidants. They have provided much insight for our large extended family. I also want to thank my sisters-in-law, Katherine Rigby, Judith Rigby, and Lois Graboys.

Those who made this book possible:

A special note of appreciation to Peter Zheutlin, lawyer turned writer. Peter brought extreme insight, sensitivity, and energy to what was a complicated endeavor. Our relationship has spanned twenty years and the intensity of the relationship has matured. Peter had to deal with those periods of time when the symptoms of the two diseases required complex writing and interpretations.

Sterling Publishing, especially my editor, Philip Turner, and his assistant, Iris Blasi.

My agent, Joelle Delbourgo, indefatigable and tells me she never sleeps.

Judy Foreman, health correspondent at the *Boston Globe,* who wrote the original profile detailing what was happening to me.

Jennifer Weis—a much appreciated and earliest supporter.

Patricia Gift—an early and valued editor.

The physicians and staff at the Lown Cardiovascular Center and the Lown Cardiovascular Research Foundation for whose support I remain humbled:

Dr. Bernard Lown—my mentor for thirty years as physician and friend. I will be forever grateful for all your support and guidance through the years.

My four associates at the Lown Cardiovascular Center—Dr. Shmuel Ravid, Dr. Charles Blatt, Dr. Brian Bilchik, and Dr. Craig Vinch. I am grateful for their patience, insight and sensitivity during this ordeal.

Helene Glaser—for nearly thirty-five years I relied on her clinical acumen, and total attention to the care and caring of our patients.

Claudia Kenney—trusted assistant over the past quarter century.

Joanne Laptewicz Ryan—able to juggle and "multi-task" while "running the show" at the Lown Center.

Carole Nathan—Executive Director of the Lown Foundation. Completely dedicated and devoted to the success of this project.

Catherine Coleman—Editor-in-Chief, Programme on Cardiovascular Health in the Developing World (ProCOR), based at the Lown Center.

The doctors who have cared for me so fervently:

Dr. Susan Block—Professor of Medicine, Harvard Medical School, whose gentle and loving understanding and encouragement have made it possible to keep rising in the morning.

Dr. John Growdon—Professor of Neurology, Harvard Medical School.

Dr. Lewis Sudarsky—Professor of Neurology at the Brigham and Women's Hospital and very concerned physician who helped guide the management of my care.

The devoted friends who have laughed and cried with me through these years:

Howard Zinn—an early enthusiastic supporter; Martha Crowninshield—a major "player" in this project and earliest supporter of the book; Marty Linsky and Lyn Staley—devoted friends over these past decades; John Spooner—sage counsel and wry humorist; Jeffrey and Susan Sussman, Roger Levy; Dr. John Rutherford—Professor of Medicine, University of Texas. Dr. Gilbert Mudge—my closest supporter over the past thirty years at the Brigham; Dr. David Greer—retired Dean of the Brown University School of Medicine and my very first mentor who introduced me to Bernard Lown; and so many others too numerous to list.

The team that continues to care every day for my physical and emotional needs:

The entire crew at the Newton Center Peet's coffee shop—without a daily latte it would be difficult to fly through the clouds; Alex Klemmer and Bill Pryor at Spynergy; Emily Savard and Brad Sullivan—my personal trainers; Danielle Trembley—my physical and massage therapist; Chanel Luck—my yoga instructor.

Susie McIntosh—friend and special assistant who has infinite patience with me; Lydia Alfonso, the glue that holds our household together; Pam Piantedosi—organizer, bill payer and computer wiz; Holli Van Nest—cook extraordinaire.

Index

ABOUT THE AUTHORS

THOMAS B. GRABOYS, M.D., is professor of medicine at Harvard Medical School, President Emeritus of the Lown Cardiovascular Research Foundation in Brookline, Massachuchetts, and Senior Physician at Brigham and Women's Hospital in Boston. During his thirty-year career, he has been widely regarded as one of Boston's leading cardiologists, and has been published extensively in the scientific literature. In 1985, Dr. Graboys was part of the team of doctors who won the Nobel Peace Prize for their work with the International Physicians for the Prevention of Nuclear War. Parkinson's disease and dementia forced his premature retirement from active clinical practice in 2006. Dr. Graboys lives in Boston with his wife, Vicki Tenney Graboys.

PETER ZHEUTLIN is a freelance journalist whose work has appeared in the *Boston Globe,* the *Christian Science Monitor, The New York Times, AARP Magazine,* and dozens of other newspapers and magazines in the United States and abroad. He is the author of *Around the World on Two Wheels: Annie Londonderry's Extraordinary Ride* (Citadel Press, 2007).